DISCIPLINING YOUR PRESCHOOLER

and
Feeling Good About It

ALSO BY MITCH AND SUSAN GOLANT

- *Kindergarten: It Isn't What It Used to Be*
- *Getting Through to Your Kids*
- *Finding Time for Fathering*
- *What to Do When Someone You Love is Depressed*

OTHER BOOKS BY MITCH GOLANT, PH.D.

- *Sometimes It's OK to Be Angry!* (with Bob Crane)
- *It's OK to Be Shy!* (with Bob Crane)
- *It's OK to Be Different!* (with Bob Crane)
- *Sometimes It's OK to Be Afraid!* (with Bob Crane)
- *The Challenging Child* (with Donna Corwin)

OTHER BOOKS BY SUSAN K. GOLANT, M.A.

- *How to Have a Smarter Baby*
  (with Dr. Susan Ludington-Hoe)
- *No More Hysterectomies* (with Vicki Hufnagel, M.D.)
- *The Joys and Challenges of Raising a Gifted Child*
- *Hardball for Women* (with Dr. Pat Heim)
- *Smashing the Glass Ceiling* (with Pat Heim, Ph.D.)
- *50 Ways to Keep Your Child Safe*
- *Kangaroo Care* (with Dr. Susan Ludington-Hoe)
- *Taking Charge: Overcoming the Eight Fears of Chronic Illness* (with Irene Pollin, M.S.W.)
- *Helping Yourself Help Others* (with Rosalynn Carter)
- *The Batterer: A Psychological Profile*
  (with Don Dutton, Ph.D.)

DISCIPLINING YOUR PRESCHOOLER

and
Feeling Good About It

■ ■ ■

MITCH GOLANT, PH.D
AND
SUSAN K. GOLANT

THIRD EDITION

LOWELL HOUSE

LOS ANGELES

CONTEMPORARY BOOKS

CHICAGO

Library of Congress Cataloging-in-Publication Data

Golant, Mitch.
  Disciplining your preschooler and feeling good about it.
    Bibliography: p.
    Includes index.
     1. Discipline of children—United States.
2. Parenting—United States. I. Golant, Susan K.
II. Title.
HQ770.4.G65   989   649.64   89–2758
ISBN 1-56565-809-4 (third edition)

            Lowell House
            2020 Avenue of the Stars, Suite 300
            Los Angeles, CA 90067

Lowell House books can be purchased at special discounts when ordered
in bulk for premiums and special sales.

Publisher: Jack Artenstein
Associate Publisher, Lowell House Adult: Bud Sperry
Director of Publishing Services: Rena Copperman
Managing Editor: Maria Magallanes
Text Design: Robert S. Tinnon

Manufactured in the United States of America
10 9 8 7 6 5 4 3 2

Contents

13,45

To our children, who made it all possible

To the Parents of Preschoolers

FEELING GOOD about discipline? It sounds like a contradiction in terms. How could anything so difficult and potentially painful make you feel good? Disciplining usually means problems, and problems mean tears, tantrums, and frustration. What are we, sadists? Whom are we trying to kid?

Well, we're here to break the myth that being a disciplinarian is tantamount to being an ogre or "the bad guy." It is possible to discipline your preschooler and feel good about it. In fact, with effective and appropriate discipline, you enhance closeness in your family and increase love. We are going to help you understand the basics of disciplining your child with love so that he or she and you—in fact your whole family—will be happier and your lives more harmonious. Along the way, we hope to support you in putting up with some of the discomforts of child-raising.

It sounds like a tough order, and it can be if you've gotten used to certain patterns of response and behavior that make disciplining difficult. But there are many steps that you, as a responsible parent, can take to create a system of caring that actually works for your family.

And that's why we have written this book. We realize that you don't want to repeat the mistakes your own parents made. You hope your kids won't be plagued with the problems that you experienced in growing up. Yet you feel trapped between your past and a certain sense of perfectionism about the "proper" approach to parenting with all of its attendant anxieties. Mistakes and missteps loom as disasters of major proportions. Some of our friends have even postponed child bearing indefinitely or until they are "ready," because they fear not knowing how to handle their child when the going gets rough.

That kind of anxiety is understandable, yet it is unnecessary. Throughout the pages of this book, we will be sharing with you our own struggles and difficulties as we raised our children. Sometimes we're amazed that with all of our errors, our family has thrived. In fact, we believe that the mistakes we made helped us become better parents because they pushed us to deal with not only our children's issues but with our own. We learned from our mistakes, and we hope that you, too, will be able to benefit from our example.

WHO ARE WE?

We speak from both professional and personal experience. We are a husband-and-wife team—Dr. Mitch Golant, a clinical psychologist who has successfully treated hundreds of families in his private practice, and Susan Golant, the coauthor of books on parenting and medical-and-social issues. We also are the father and mother of two (grown, thank God) daughters. Between both girls, we have pulled off 50 birthday parties. That's a lot of cake and candles! And, believe us, that's also many years of parental mistakes and family conflicts to resolve.

Although our children are "out of the nest," we are just verging on fifty. Yes, unlike the rest of our peer group, we started young. We understand the concerns of parents today because we are of the same generation, yet we have already gone through the wars. When people hear that our daughters are out of college, they stare at us in shocked disbelief. In fact, we're pretty shocked about it ourselves. On the other hand, many of our friends with preschoolers come to us for advice since they know we've been there and have survived. We hope to be able to help you in much the same way.

HOW THIS BOOK IS SET UP

Disciplining Your Preschooler and Feeling Good About It is divided into three parts. Part One, "Getting Ready," helps you understand why your preschooler wants and needs discipline, even though he may act as if he doesn't. We explore the virtues of structure and the notion that you can undo all of your well-laid plans by harboring unrealistic expectations for your children. Part Two, "Essential Elements of Disciplining with Love," covers setting limits, testing, the value of family meetings, the importance of appropriate consequences, consistency and follow-through, and the use of positive reinforcement and humor to change behavior. We also show you how to present a united front to your child, even if you and your spouse have differing parenting styles. In Part Three, we cover the "Thorny Problems" of tantrums, lying, sibling conflicts, spanking, and disciplining in the two-career family.

Each chapter closes with the Feeling-Good-About-Discipline Program, our step-by-step guide to helping you cope with your preschooler's behavior.

WHAT TO WATCH OUT FOR

In thinking and writing about our own lives in the context of the research on child development and Mitch's clinical experience with many families over the years, we have become aware that certain themes repeat themselves in families dealing with discipline issues. In fact, as you read this book, you will find at least six key ideas that weave throughout the chapters. We introduce these ideas to you at the outset because we feel that they are crucial to your coming to grips with discipline issues within your family:

1. *Playing the role of "the good guy."* Many parents want their children to like them. This is understandable. You love your children, and you want them to love you back. Yet some parents hesitate to discipline their children fearing that their kids will resent the restrictions.

It hurts, of course, when your preschooler yells, "I hate you," after you have sent her to her room for a time-out. But there are ways of dealing with her anger that let her know that although you appreciate her distress, she still needs to follow the rules you've set down. Sometimes playing "the good guy" gets you into more trouble than setting forth the limits and sticking to them. Kids want and need discipline. We'll discuss many examples of this throughout the book, but especially in Chapters 1, 6, and 13.

2. *Discipline is a long-term goal.* Discipline can be looked at as a last-ditch, I'm-at-the-end-of-my-rope, you-deserve-this-because-you've-been-bad gut reaction to your child's behavior. This springs from your frustration with the preschooler's unwillingness to follow your rules. Such reactive discipline may hurt more than it helps. We would like you to approach discipline as a long-term goal for your family. It's a way of relating. You create structure and safety within your family by setting limits and keeping to them. (There is more on this in Chapters 2, 3, 5, 6, and 14.) Discipline as structure enhances your child's self-esteem and feelings of security.

3. *Disciplining children also means discipline for parents.* This is a tough one. Children learn by example. They are quick to sense when your words and actions don't match and equally quick to point out that you've been hypocritical. If, for ex-

ample, you don't want your kids to smoke, don't lecture to them about the perils of tobacco with a cigarette dangling from your lips. This also goes for dealing with stealing, lying, cheating, drinking, using drugs, and so on. You can't expect to teach your child values that you don't *practice* yourself. When preschoolers become teenagers (they all do, eventually, you know), they'll throw all of your vices in your face with a vengeance. "Do as I say . . ." never works.

In addition, parental discipline means putting up with new ways of coping, which may feel unfamiliar and difficult to you. At various moments in the text, we have pointed out when something we suggest may take some discipline on your part. Understand that this is difficult for all parents and that it is part of the struggle to come to grips with your own past. You'll find more on this in Chapter 6, in particular.

4. *Parenting involves reliving your own childhood.* In one way or another, it is inevitable that you will replay with your children some old scenes from your own growing-up experience. Everyone does this. After all, you have only your own life experiences to go by. In fact, the greatest predictor of how you treat your children is how you yourself were treated as a child.

When you are aware of the role that your family's behavior plays in your actions as a parent today, you can take steps to do things differently than your parents did with you. Sometimes, however, those patterns of behavior are so ingrained or even unconscious that you haven't a clue as to where they've come from. Working out these issues while you raise your preschooler is one of the challenges of parenthood. Information in Chapters 9 and 12 may help you in this area.

5. *Discipline often means changing behavior.* Many times when we talk about discipline, we mean making a child stop a hurtful activity, such as throwing sand at the playground or rejecting a sibling. We may also wish to replace the negative behavior with something more positive, such as cooperation. In Chapters 7 and 8, we cover how to use positive rein-

forcement and humor to make those changes. And throughout the book, we share other techniques that will help you
to modify your preschooler's behavior, especially when it
comes to tantrums and sibling arguments. (See Chapters 10
and 12 for tips on these.)

6. *Have the courage to admit to yourself and to your child that
you've overreacted or otherwise made a mistake.* Despite our fantasies to the contrary, life is not a progression from one peak
experience to the next. Everyone makes mistakes; everyone suffers from doubt; and everyone flies off the handle
once in a while. That's normal. We all certainly made some
lulus, as you'll soon see. The trick is to recognize when you've
gone too far and then make amends to your child. Rather
than diminishing your status in your child's eyes when you
admit to a mistake, your honesty and responsibility will ren-
der you more human to him.

Bear in mind that despite the fact that your son is little
and you're quite big, you are both people just struggling to
make it through another day. When you apologize, you
demonstrate to your child your deep respect for him as a fel-
low human being, and he feels honored by your considera-
tion of his feelings. This act builds trust and love.

Taken together, all of these ideas form the backbone of
Disciplining Your Preschooler and Feeling Good About It. They
are the principles upon which our work is based.

Are we ready? So now, with our apologies to Maurice
Sendak, illustrious author of *Where the Wild Things Are* (Max
is the quintessential—and our daughters' favorite—literary
preschooler), *let the wild rumpus begin!*

PART ONE

Getting Ready

CHAPTER ONE

It's Like the Tail Wagging the Dog

Why Children Want and Need Discipline

WE DROPPED IN to see our friend Mindy and found her locked in a familiar struggle with her four-year-old, Angela. Mindy had rented a videotape of the movie *Cinderella*, thinking that Angela would enjoy watching something new. Well, Angela had others plans altogether. Her heart was set on viewing *Dumbo* for the fortieth time and no amount of pleading or cajoling on her mother's part would get her to accept the film offered. In fact, just as we came through the door, Angela had thrown herself onto the den couch and was kicking at the upholstered arms as hard as she could, screaming as if her life were endangered.

Poor Mindy was a wreck. She was embarrassed that we had witnessed such a scene of unbridled and uncontrolled rage on the part of her mostly perfect daughter. She felt angry. She felt helpless. And worst of all, she was on the verge of jumping into the car and driving across town to seek out the *Dumbo* tape just to quiet the tantrum.

She turned to us in desperation. "What should I do?" she whispered. "She just won't stop. I can't stand it when she cries like that, and she knows it. I'm at my wits' end."

Clearly, this was a case of the tail wagging the dog.

THE TAIL WAGGING THE DOG

What a funny expression. But that's exactly how it feels when your preschooler is in control of you—and not the reverse:

- She is whiny and manipulative.
- She is demanding.
- She throws tantrums when she doesn't get her way.
- She knows how to insinuate herself between her mother and her father, and plays one parent against the other—causing marital as well as family discord.

Undisciplined or ineffectually disciplined kids can be the little tyrants who disrupt family weddings, kick the housekeeper or hurt a younger sibling. They dawdle maddeningly when it's time for nursery school, causing you to be late for work, or worse yet, they refuse to go to school altogether. They run amok in the supermarket, pulling forbidden sweets from shelves and letting out bloodcurdling screams when you won't purchase what they fancy. They won't clean up their rooms, no matter how many times you ask or how loudly you yell. They present nightly difficulties at bedtime, refusing to go to sleep, especially with a sitter. They won't take "No" for an answer and pester you with the perennial "Why?"—a bane of parents—when you won't give in to their demands.

At his worst, an unruly and manipulative preschooler will grow into a surly, aggressive, and intimidating child. Such kids adjust poorly to living in our society. They

- continue to shriek, scream, and tantrum beyond preschool years.
- hurt small animals and other people.
- can't be taken anywhere.
- destroy property.
- refuse to cooperate.
- won't take responsibility for their negative acts and blame everyone else.
- bully their peers; they have few friends.
- constantly run into discipline problems with school authorities.

Of course, this is a worst case scenario but one that is frightening, nonetheless. Even your "normal" child, however, can give you a pain in the neck. As much as you love your kids, you may find them loud and obnoxious and at times unbearable to live with. We are reminded of a *Calvin and Hobbes* cartoon strip. Five-year-old Calvin has wandered away from his parents during an outing at the zoo. They look for him frantically. Finally Calvin's father decides to search a wider area. He walks off, gritting his teeth as he mutters, "Being a parent is wanting to hug and strangle your kid at the same time." Haven't we all had that feeling? You love them, but, boy, they can be exasperating sometimes.

The truth is, kids who have not been appropriately and lovingly disciplined find it rough going once they become adolescents and adults. It may be hard for them to make and keep friends, because they've never learned about cooperation and sharing. They insist on being the center of attention at all times. They can have unrealistic expectations of the people around them and anticipate that their every desire will be satisfied. Or they are perpetual complainers that the world has not treated them right. Yet they can be oblivious to the needs of those around them and insensitive to hurting others' feelings.

The trick here is to reassert your authority as *parents*. You are the ones who are in charge of the family. You call the shots. You set the rules for everyone's safety and comfort. Some decisions are just not up to your preschooler. He may not like it, but that's the way life is. Here's how we helped our friend Mindy come to grips with this issue.

ESTABLISHING WHO'S IN CHARGE

Back to the videotape. As in all families, there were many factors contributing to Mindy's situation. To begin with, Angela was a desperately wanted child—one who came into the lives of Mindy and Rich after years of infertility problems. Angela's parents would do *anything* to make her happy. That's understandable. She was the answer to their most cherished desire.

Yet in the process, Mindy had surrendered too much power to her daughter. Unwilling to see her cry for any reason, Mindy gave in to Angela's demands. And the four-year-old, naturally, got used to having the upper hand with her forty-year-old mother. Rich was no better off. He was entirely enchanted by his daughter, and she had him wrapped around her finger. Angela had a great thing going and didn't want to let it go. Could you blame her?

When we walked in on Mindy and Angela, however, our gut response was instantaneous and unanimous. There was something terribly unbalanced about the scene before us. Since our friend had asked for help, we felt safe in speaking up before her problem became more serious. We posed several questions:

- Why would you put yourself out to get another videotape?

- What message would that convey to your child?
- Where and when is this going to stop?
- What would it be like to tell Angela that *Cinderella* is the tape you rented and that she can watch it or nothing at all since you're not going out to the store to get another one?

This was a new approach for Mindy, and one that felt uncomfortable to her. But she was willing to try it because she felt desperate. With a little coaching, she was ready to return to "the lion's den." She started the tape in the VCR and talked to Angela through her screams. "I know you wanted to watch *Dumbo*, but we have *Cinderella* today," she said, firmly. "I'm not willing to go out and get another tape now. You can watch this or nothing at all. Next time, when I return this tape, I'll get you *Dumbo*."

We can't say that this new approach worked instantly or perfectly. After having been in control for so long, Angela was not ready to give up the reins or be mollified by her mother's assurances. Her kicks and screams redoubled as the film began. Truly, she sounded as if she were being beaten to within seconds of her life. She held her hands over her ears and closed her eyes. She turned red as a radish. We walked out of the room, pulling Mindy with us. We were not going to reinforce Angela's behavior with our presence or reaction.

Mindy was anguished. She worried that she was permanently scarring her child by causing this much unhappiness. We reassured her that crying is a useful way for kids to vent their own frustrations. After all, Mindy was not depriving Angela of food or love or anything else that was vital. She was not hurting her in any way. She simply had set up a reasonable limit of what she was willing to do in terms of a recreation. If there was to be any peace at all in their household, Angela was going to have to learn to live within the limits that her parents had created, and her parents were going to have to learn to assert themselves and to put up with Angela's frustration.

WHY LIMITS ARE IMPORTANT

We all live with socially imposed limitations on our behavior. Imagine if none of us wanted to stop at a red light or if we all decided to take what we wanted, whether it belonged to us or not. Life would be strife-ridden and terribly chaotic. We abide by certain socially acceptable rules that we have imposed on ourselves for our own good and the good of the community. Our rules provide for our safety and well-being.

A family is also a form of community. Every family has rules or limits. Some are spoken, and some are simply understood. Limits teach children important lessons about the world and promote safety. They provide kids with a feeling of security. Jason must hold your hand while crossing the street. He must not talk to strangers. He must keep his hands off the hot stove and away from steamy cups of coffee. He must not poke the cat in the eye or pull the dog's tail. No playing with knives. No playing with matches. No biting. No pinching. No hair pulling. These are limits that you impose every day.

Limits are what transform your child from a mass of quivering protoplasm into a human being who functions in our society. Social psychologists, those who devote their lives to studying how babies actually become little human beings, have delineated the areas where children must learn to abide by limits and rules set by their families and the society around them. These problems of *socialization* are shared by all cultures and all societies in the world. They include rules and limits relating to

- eating.
- excreting.

- sexuality.
- aggression.
- dependence and independence.
- emotional development and attachment to others.
- achievement.
- competition and cooperation.
- sense of individuality.
- life and death.
- mating.
- pain.
- right and wrong.

We have rules about all of these areas: what's OK and what's not OK. Take the massive numbers of rules we have learned to live by in just the first category. We eat with a fork and knife or a spoon from clean plates; we chew our food with our mouths closed; we keep our elbows off the table; even the fact that we sit at a table and don't squat on the floor is important. The limits and rules vary from family to family, region to region, culture to culture, but they exist everywhere people come into contact with other people.

Our task as parents is to teach our children how to fit into the limits and rules that are acceptable to our family and our society. One of our teaching tools is discipline. With discipline, we assert to our children what is acceptable and what is unacceptable in their behavior.

When our preschoolers make "unreasonable demands" (unreasonable for our culture, that is), the role of limit setting and discipline is to help corral them back into socially acceptable behavior. If we give in to their unreasonable demands, we may be making it harder for them to become socialized and, in the long run, may hurt them more than it helps them.

Some parents feel that if they set limits, they are squelching their children's independence and individuality. This is a paradoxical problem. In actuality, giving children free rein makes them more dependent. How? When we don't take charge, our children perceive that it's our job to fulfill their every need. They have not learned how to channel their frustrations constructively or how to comfort themselves when thwarted.

Indeed, children of permissive parents often feel that their Mom and Dad weren't concerned enough about them to set up rules. These kids attempt more and more outrageous acts as a cry for attention and the safety of structure.

We encountered such a family one day while we were picnicking at the park. A father was holding his three-year-old daughter in his arms as he drank from a bottle of beer. The child began pulling at the bottle and yelling. The father gave in to his daughter's demand and let her have a sip. He laughed at her response to the alcoholic beverage. She liked it and wanted more.

Rather than putting the beer away, the father told the little girl that he wouldn't give her anymore. She didn't like this and cried and screamed until he gave in and let her have another sip. When he refused her a third taste, she became more disruptive. She knocked the bottle out of his hand, splashing them both with the brew. He yelled at her, telling her what a bad girl she was for spilling his beer.

It was a sad scene to witness. This young child wanted something that was unreasonable, but her father had not created an atmosphere where limit setting could be achieved appropriately.

WANTS AND NEEDS

The little girl at the picnic *wanted* the beer. Indeed, we all have wants and needs and demands of ourselves and others. Our children are certainly entitled to theirs. When they express their wants, it helps them to feel powerful and in control of their lives. This is an important part of their learning how to get along with others. And, as a parent, you certainly wouldn't want your child to be too meek or frightened to ask for what he needs from you or from other people.

We want to please our child by granting him his wants and needs. We want to play "the good guy" and feel the pressure to do what is right for our child. Sometimes we feel that our child knows best what he himself wants or needs. That's fine.

On the other hand, sometimes our child's wants and needs step outside the bounds of what is possible or acceptable. Then we are faced with a conflict. Our child's want and needs become a problem when

- we feel they are unreasonable, and yet we perceive them as an *order* that we must obey.
- he's impinging on the rights of another (for example, if he's hitting his baby brother on the head with his favorite Transformer).
- his desires may be perfectly reasonable but we don't want to fulfill them because we've run out of time, energy, money, patience, or whatever.

A BIRD IN THE HAND . . .

An ancient Chinese tale illustrates the value of limits for parents. The Buddha was teaching his followers and students. He held a bird on his outstretched palm. Members of the assembled group tried to mimic their teacher's feat. Yet each time one of them attempted to hold the bird, it flew away.

Intrigued, one of the students asked the sage how he had managed when they had all failed. The Buddha replied, "Each of us needs a platform from which to take off. I drop my hand each time the bird makes the motion to fly. He has nothing to push away from."

This story is instructive in two seemingly contradictory ways. When you drop your hand by acceding to your child's unreasonable demands, you make growing up more difficult. On the other hand, children also need a "taking-off place"—solid ground against which they can push to define who they are. By your having set limits, kids feel safer, more successful, and more contained. Even though they may act to the contrary, they know that you care enough about them to prevent them from hurting themselves. From this position, they can eventually become more independent. They can take off and soar.

THE GLASS SLIPPER, AT LAST

Back to Angela, the videotape, and the Fairy Godmother, not to mention Prince Charming at the ball. After about five minutes of all-out pandemonium, there was sudden silence in the den of Mindy and Rich's home. "Oh my God," said Mindy. "What's happened to Angela? Could she have choked herself with all that crying?"

We tiptoed back to the room, holding our breath, and peered inside. There was one very sweaty, very tired four-year-old, sucking her thumb, twirling her hair, snuffling, and sniffling but absolutely enthralled by the scene that was unfolding before her.

We crept away, knowing full well that this was only the beginning of a long and probably difficult process. But we had faith that, at least, the first step had been taken.

■ ■ ■

Feeling Good About Discipline
POINTS TO KEEP IN MIND

1. Children want and need discipline.
2. Discipline provides a feeling of safety and structure.
3. Undisciplined children find it hard to get along with others as they grow to maturity.
4. Children of permissive parents attempt more and more outrageous acts as a way of gaining the security of structure.
5. Limits help children to become responsible members of society.
6. We all have wants and needs, but sometimes our children's wants and needs are inappropriate.
7. Parents need to assert their role as parents in order to take charge. Being "the good guy" often doesn't help.
8. Children need a "taking-off place" in order to soar.

CHAPTER TWO

Green Peas in Cambria

Unreasonable Expectations and Parental Frustration

THE FANTASY

We had mapped out a perfect vacation for ourselves. We anticipated driving up the coast from our home in Los Angeles. Our eventual destination was Yosemite via the romantic village of Carmel. Along the way we planned to stop at San Simeon to tour the Hearst Castle, a famous California attraction. We had reservations on the 1:00 P.M. tour. One of our still childless friends had recommended the names of some great restaurants, and we were expecting to have a marvelous time.

One problem. We forgot to take into account that we were bringing along an eighteen-month-old and a five-year-old.

How could we have made such an oversight? That's easy! We just hadn't thought the vacation through to its logical conclusion. It was something we wanted to do, and we figured the kids would go along with it. We practiced denial—that is, we didn't want our plans to be a problem so we acted as if they weren't. In the process, we had forgotten to take our kids' needs into account. In other words, we made a big mistake.

Our error served to remind us once more that parenting is a difficult job, perhaps the most difficult one we will ever be asked to perform. It is a balancing act in which we must try to create some kind of equilibrium between our own needs and those of our children.

These decisions come up daily in all of our lives. You want some quiet time, and they want to play horsie. They're ready for a nap, and you must leave for a two o'clock pediatrician's appointment. You want a structured, memorable vacation filled with sight-seeing at castles and elaborate, romantic, candlelit dinners, and they can handle only *building* their own sand castles at the beach and Big Macs and fries at McDonald's. These conflicting needs and the resolutions that you work out make up the day-to-day fabric of your family routine.

Sometimes it's hard to know the right thing to do. If this is your first child, or if your extended family is unavailable for advice (or if you believe that your own parents did it all wrong), you may not know how to proceed when the going gets rough. Having never been a parent before, you don't know if you're doing the right thing. You have no previous experience to guide you. You watch your friends for cues, but they may be no better off than you. The truth is, it's difficult to be a good parent in today's society.

You are bombarded by conflicting messages from books, television, and magazines.

You may live far from grandparents, parents, aunts, and uncles who can offer some guidance.

You may be consumed by work or financial pressures and

find it difficult to create the time and peace necessary to spend with your child.

You may feel intimidated by the superparent image that seems to prevail in today's media.

It's only natural that you will make mistakes. We did—and quite often, at that. One of the biggest was that trip. It wasn't that our kids had made unreasonable demands on us, rather, we just had unreasonable expectations of them.

THE REALITY

It's a four-hour drive from Los Angeles to San Simeon. Allowing for pit stops and lunch, we figured we had to leave early. And we did. We were up at 6:00 A.M. and out by 7:00.

When we arrived at San Simeon (just barely in time for the tour), we sped from the car to the bus that was to take us up the narrow, winding road to the castle. Once we got there, we strapped Aimee, our youngest, into her stroller. Cherie, at five, could certainly walk, but she, as well as all tourists, had to be confined to the cordoned pathways through the ornate rooms. There was no touching of *anything*.

Of course, after about an hour, the usual litany began: "I'm hungry." "I'm thirsty." "I need to go to the bathroom." "My feet hurt." "How much longer do we have to stay?" "When can we go home?" We couldn't just leave. We had to wait for the tour to end and take the bus back down the hill.

Our toddler, who had now been railroaded through her naptime, was becoming ultracrabby. She pushed, kicked, and squirmed, trying to get herself out of bondage. Who could blame her? She had been a virtual prisoner of our plans since 7:00 that morning.

We endured another hour or so of torture, and then finally we were given a reprieve when the tour bus brought us back down to our car. But our problems weren't over.

After a brief nap at a motel in the neighboring town of Cambria, we dressed up and went to dinner at one of the recommended restaurants. Our friend was right. It really was a lovely place. Fine Persian rugs covered the floors, the tables were set with expensive and exquisite antique china and crystal, and the menu was French. It was great!

By the time our entrées arrived, however, the kids were fit to be tied. With unrepressed giggling and loud shrieks of glee, they proceeded to roll green peas on the fine table linens and finished by flinging the peas at us, each other, and the surrounding well-dressed restaurant patrons. No amount of dirty looks or shushing between clenched teeth made a difference to them. It was time to play fast and loose, and they were going to go for it. The waiters rolled their eyes at us. We were certain they were thinking, "What bratty, undisciplined kids!" To an outsider, it sure seemed that way.

"TO AVOID PERVERSION, ALLOW DIVERSION"

Over the years, we had developed a tactic that helped us to get through difficult times with the kids. The motto, To Avoid Perversion, Allow Diversion, was first applied when Cherie was about ten months old. She had pulled herself up to a standing position while holding on to our bookcases that were suspended on ceiling-to-floor tension poles. In that stance, she gingerly tossed one book after the other over her shoulder while calling out "No, no, no!" in a singsong voice. It was obvious to us that telling her no in this instance was just not going to work. So, instead, we diverted her attention with a collection of blocks and cups that she could build and destroy. Our scheme worked!

We found this motto helpful on many occasions afterward and would recite it to each other at moments just like these and then take some appropriate action. What were the diversionary tactics in Cambria? Each of us took turns walking one of the kids outside in the parking lot while the other parent and child gulped down dinner. Most assuredly, this was not the evening we had anticipated. Our perfectly prepared beef Wellingtons were ruined: The pastry got cold and tasted gummy, and the steak, once tender, had turned to tepid chewing gum that we struggled to swallow. But at least we got through the meal without further raucous outbursts.

NO ONE IS TO BLAME, AND NO ONE IS PERFECT

Our vacation had gotten off to a very poor start, and we were disappointed. That's important. Disappointment over thwarted expectations undermines family closeness and enjoyment of one another. It's the source of anger and frustration and can lead to arguments and accusations.

Children want to please their parents, and they feel badly if they don't meet parental expectations—no matter how unreasonable those expectations may be. How many times have we heard "You made Mommy angry. That was a bad thing to do" and see the child shrivel inside? Yet our expectations may not fit the reality. Our preschoolers are not going to be on their best behavior when they're sleepy and need a nap. They may not cooperate in a setting that requires them to sit quietly without the opportunity for wiggling or exploring for long periods of time.

It's important to pay attention to how your family deals with problems when things don't go as planned or, as in our case, when they become disastrous. Sometimes a problem between husband and wife will get taken out on the kids. Recriminations fly. "I never wanted to do this. You made me." "Why don't you ever take responsibility?" "Can't you get those kids to shut up?" These attitudes can be destructive and can get in the way of your figuring out what actually went wrong and how to prevent the problem from recurring the next time out.

Sometimes it's helpful to realize that no one was to blame. Whatever you had planned was a good idea that just didn't work. There's no guilt and no blame. You make mistakes, and you learn. We certainly made our share. In fact, the purpose of this chapter is to show you not how to eliminate errors, but that they are a natural part of life. We want to help you recognize when your child is misbehaving as a result of your unrealistic (and perhaps unreasonable) expectations and how you can deal with the same situation more comfortably in the future.

WHAT ABOUT OUR RUINED DINNER?

Was it true that the kids were bratty and undisciplined? Were we doing a poor job of keeping them in line?

Not knowing the context of our day, you might be able to make a case for that point of view—the waiter certainly did. But late that evening, as we whispered about the events of the day over the soft, sweet breathing of sleeping children, we came to the conclusion that the embarrassment was not their problem. It was ours. With our unrealistic expectations, we had created an impossible situation that left us all angry and frustrated.

Should we never take them to dinner at a nice restaurant? Absolutely not! It wasn't the dinner that did them in. It was the whole day of confinement and restraint. They didn't have a chance to run around and let off excess energy. When did they have an opportunity to be just kids? They were forced to a timetable that was difficult even for adults. Plus we didn't take their limited attention spans into account. We weren't being fair to our kids, and it spoiled the day for all of us.

How could we have improved the situation? We might have

planned to do less. We might have divided the leg of the trip to Cambria over two days. Day one, we travel. Day two, we spend the morning at the castle and the afternoon at the beach and napping. By dinnertime, we would be rested, refreshed, and ready to behave properly. Most important, we hadn't done our homework. We should have informed ourselves of the nature of the tour. Had we known that there was a shuttle bus and we would not be able to return to our car until the tour had ended, we might have planned accordingly.

So after leaving San Simeon, we jettisoned our friend's wonderful dining guide and stuck to Bob's Big Boy until we got to Yosemite. Not the healthiest fare or the most elegant ambience, but the kids could spill their milk, drop ketchupy French fries on the seat, and giggle to their heart's content. We had a much better time after that. And we all learned our lesson.

WHAT TO EXPECT FROM YOUR PRESCHOOLER

Perhaps our vacation would have been planned more realistically if we had had a better understanding of child development. Preschoolers are not equipped to respond to the needs of others. Developmental psychologists, including Margaret Mahler, Erik Erikson, and Jean Piaget, have explored the stages that children go through as they reach maturity. It's important to bear in mind the major points of their research so that you don't create situations that are frustrating for your family as well:

1. *Early childhood is a time when children gain psychological and physical separateness from parents.* In moving from a state of being fused with her parents during infancy to seeing her parents as a separate entity, your child begins to regulate her

own emotional and physical life. She feeds herself, dresses herself, and becomes happy or angry at her parents because she sees them as people distinct from herself. She can tell them, "No!"

2. *Children are still "egocentric."* Preschoolers cannot take the point of view of others. Their world revolves around themselves. For example, when we wanted to look at the artwork in Hearst Castle, Cherie was hungry and tired. She didn't care about our needs. In effect Cherie, like most kids, wanted what she wanted when she wanted it.

3. *Conflicts between self-centered desires and the needs of others occur.* You can see how this idea follows from the first and second. If we as parents are different from our children, then their needs won't necessarily be our needs. They most likely won't take our needs into account, because they don't know how to do that just yet. In fact, it doesn't even enter their minds to think about us and our needs—nor are they supposed to. That's one of the reasons why tantrums occur.

4. *The sense of conscience begins to occur.* At this point, your child begins to feel guilt for something that he has done wrong. But he doesn't feel that he needs to do anything to change himself. That's why when kids say, "I'm sorry Mommy, I didnot want to step on the flowers," and seem to mean it, they think nothing of doing it again the next time they're in the yard playing ball! Even more frustrating, they profess to be just as sorry the next time.

5. *Language develops.* Between the ages of two and seven, children begin to use language as a powerful tool. They now have the ability to engage in what's called *symbolic play*. That is, a broomstick would make a marvelous horse for riding around the house. They manipulate images and make up stories. This becomes important if you're concerned about lying (see Chapter 11).

DO PRESCHOOLERS KNOW THE DIFFERENCE BETWEEN RIGHT AND WRONG?

Babies are born in a state of innocent bliss. They have no sense of morals at all. An important part of our job as parents is to teach our developing children right and wrong, good and bad, shalts and shalt nots. The hope is that once we convey to our children the moral values that we feel are important, they will "internalize" them—that is, they will make them a part of their own code of action and ethics. In that way, they will grow into responsible adults, capable of participating in society.

Do preschoolers have a sense of wrong and right? The answer is no! Not yet. According to the renowned Swiss developmental psychologist, Jean Piaget, children are not even aware of rules at this time in their lives. For example, they may play with marbles or checkers because they like to handle them, not because they want to win the game. Even if at the age of four or five they become aware of rules from observing an older brother or sister, they still don't understand what the concept of rules means.

So how, then, is your preschooler's behavior governed? The developmental psychologist Dr. L. Kohlberg has studied moral development intensely. He has come up with the theory that a preschooler determines whether an act is good or bad based on that action's immediate consequence to *him*. He will obey a parent in order to avoid punishment. On the other hand, if he can "get away" with something then the act isn't bad, since he as received no punishment for it.

For example, four-year-old Aimee once took a pack of gum from the supermarket, thinking that it was hers for the taking. When we arrived home, she displayed her trophy to Susan with great pride. She had no sense that she had done something wrong. Taking the gum was something to boast about; after all, she liked gum and got to have this pack all to herself. Susan explained to Aimee that it was not OK to take things from the store without paying for them, no matter how much we want them, and that when grown-ups do such things, the police can come and take them to jail. So they returned to the store and returned the pack of gum. Properly chastised by the imagined consequence of jail, Aimee never took anything from the store again.

Because your preschooler responds to consequences, your system of discipline will be based on the consequence that you establish. Simply telling your child that it's wrong to hurt his sister without creating an appropriate consequence will not be effective in changing his behavior. This is a very important point that we will be exploring more fully in the next several chapters.

WHEN AGENDAS CLASH

Not all frustrating situations are based on your preschooler's inability to distinguish right from wrong. In an excellent book entitled *How to Stop the Battle with You Child*, psychologist Don Fleming points out that "quarreling between the parents and a seemingly difficult child may simply be due to a simple misunderstanding between agendas."

He gives the example of a parent and child standing in line waiting for a movie. Although you the parent may be restless, your agenda is for your child to be quiet and cooperative. His agenda, on the other hand, is to make a boring situation more entertaining. "This might entail breaking loose from your hand, making faces, or picking fights with the kids next in line."

Dr. Fleming makes the point that your child is doing exactly what he's supposed to be doing. He's being a child! And part of the work of childhood is to explore the world in as many ways as possible. The problem becomes one of finding a way to allow your preschooler to do so in an appropriate manner without impinging on the rights of others. You need to discipline him without stifling his natural curiosity.

There are many other times when your unrealistic expectations may create discipline problems for your preschooler. Here are just a few:

- Ordering a big meal for your child when he gets full after three bites.
- Expecting to carry on an adult conversation with a friend or spouse when your child doesn't have a companion or toys to play with.
- Taking your preschooler to a movie that runs longer than an hour and a half.
- Dressing your child in lace and satin for a birthday party and expecting her to return home in pristine condition.
- Buying your child the porcelain tea set that she has been demanding with the understanding that she won't break any of the pieces.

No matter how hard you try, these situations are bound to lead to trouble. This is not to say, however, that your child can't be taken out or should always be dressed like a slob. It's a question here again of moderation and resolving conflicting "agendas."

TAKE A MINUTE

How can you assess when your agendas are going to clash? A good rule of thumb is to take a minute in front of the mirror with your preschooler:

1. Take a deep breath and close your eyes. Relax for a moment.
2. Now look at your reflections. Compare your ages and sizes.
3. Say to yourself, "I'm Aimee's mother. What are my needs? What is my agenda?"
4. Now, take the perspective of your child. Say to yourself, "I'm Susan's daughter, and I'm four years old. What are my needs? What is my agenda?"
5. See what comes up for each of you. Think about whether or not your agenda makes sense to a four-year-old. If not, see how you can adjust to make your situation more manageable.

When you become aware of the inequalities inherent in your relationship with your child, you can more easily begin to see why the process of educating him through discipline is a long-term commitment. Think about it in terms of your child's co-ordination. Remember, when he learned to walk, he often tumbled and fell. When she grasped a ball, it took time for her to learn how to throw. Similarly, it takes a long time for your preschooler to understand all the elements of discipline.

To help yourself decide if you have an agenda problem, you can ask yourself these questions:

- What are appropriate expectations of a child his age?
- Am I allowing him enough space to explore and do his own thing without impinging on others?
- Did I bring toys for the wait in line or a pencil and some paper to doodle on while we wait for our pizza to cook?
- Am I demanding more than he can handle?
- Have I allowed enough time for him to dress himself, and does he have the skills to do so?

■ Have I eliminated distractions when I want him to pay attention to something specific?

If your preschooler isn't acting in a way that you had imagined and you are beginning to feel disappointed, frustrated, and angry it is a clear case of an agenda problem. How do you deal with agenda conflicts? That depends:

1. *Anticipate the difficulty and bring along a diversion.* Friends of ours recently brought a companion along for their four-year-old when we spent a weekend together in the mountains. Our friends figured, and rightly so, that Mikie would be less apt to disturb us if he had his best friend with him as company. He felt less jealous of the time we grownups spent together because he could also be involved in meaningful play without his parents.

2. *Improvise.* This takes some creativity and patience. If you're waiting in line for a movie, for example, you can ask someone to hold your place while you take your restless son for a walk up and down the block to look at the cars.

3. *Ignore the disturbance.* This is not always possible, but sometimes ignoring your child's negative behavior helps to extinguish it. (There's more on this in the next chapter.) Suppose you're on the bus, and your child begins a tantrum before you reach your destination. Having to tough it out and not respond to the tantrum is not easy. Try to imagine the serenity of calm blue seas as you're snorkeling in Hawaii. Realize that life is difficult sometimes, and tomorrow is another day. (You can also be thankful that you don't know anyone on the bus!) We'll talk in much more depth about tantrums in Chapter 10.

4. *Change your plans.* Sometimes this in unavoidable, especially if you find that your child can't handle the situation, and it's just not going to work. Leave the party/beach/restaurant/movie theater early and go home where you can take

appropriate action. Otherwise, you'll be stuck in the kind of thinking that makes you grit your teeth and say, "We're going to have a good time even if it kills us."

5. *Use a program of limit setting, consequence, and follow-through.* Sometimes you want your preschooler to stop what he's doing in no uncertain terms. You can tell your child to stop hitting his friend in the movie line, or you will all go home. If he continues to test your limit and hits his friend again, make good on your promise. He won't like it, but at least he'll know that you mean business. We will explain this system of discipline more fully in the next chapter.

TOO MUCH OF A GOOD THING

Over the years, we have found ways to defuse potentially volatile situations. One of the most important principles to bear in mind is that your preschooler has a much shorter attention span than you. To make everyone happy, keep your activities short and sweet.

So, for example, if we decided to go to the zoo, we usually did not make an afternoon of it. Instead, we would arrive early in the morning and spend only an hour looking at perhaps the elephants, zebras, giraffes, monkeys, and rhinoceroses. And then we would go home. On the next trip, maybe the following month, we would see the lions, tigers, snakes, and birds. Subsequent visits provided time for the kangaroos, koala bears, emus, and seals. In that way, the kids didn't become bored or overtired as a result of *our* longer attention spans or our adult need to see it all. After all, we were going to the zoo for their benefit more than ours. And they were always eager to go again because we all left in high spirits.

We handled trips to Disneyland in much the same way.

Since we live in Los Angeles, we could visit the park relatively frequently. If you're visiting from out of town, of course, it is a bit more difficult. But arranging lodging at an adjacent hotel can help because you can go back to your room for breaks.

Disneyland, like most other amusement parks, is a wondrous phantasmagoria for little kids. They delight in all of the sights, sounds, and smells. But it can also be overwhelming.

We made a point of arriving early in the morning, before the masses hit the park. We usually stayed no more than an hour and a half. This may seem foolishly indulgent when you consider the price of admission. Yet we found that after 90 minutes our kids became overstimulated. They got cranky and whiny, and we all stopped having a good time. What's the point of staying longer? We can't imagine anything more depressing than dragging a screaming child around the Magic Kingdom.

Similarly, we usually did not announce our destination when we planned such a trip. In the morning, we would let the children know that we were going out for a ride. We would reveal that this was a surprise trip only about ten minutes before we had reached our destination, during which time the excitement would build in the car as the girls tried to guess where we were taking them.

This approach helps to avoid the nagging that precedes any special occasion. Kids have a harder time than adults do in delaying gratification. If you've been assailed with hours of "When are we going to the circus?" ("Next week" or "Tuesday, the ninth" doesn't have much meaning to a preschooler) and endless repetitions of "Are we there yet?" you will understand the virtues of this approach. In a way, too much anticipation also takes the fun out of the event.

A SMASHING BIRTHDAY BASH

Speaking of keeping it short and sweet. . . . Perhaps worse than inviting too many kids to your four-year-old's birthday is allowing the party to go on for too long. Two hours is more than any group of preschoolers (and their harried parents) can handle.

Here's the aftermath of one such mistake at our house:

- The piñata hung for an hour and a half in the sun.
- The Milky Ways and Snickers inside the piñata melted.
- The kids were too small and too weak to break the piñata, so they pounded at it for more than 15 minutes, rendering whatever solid candy inside to mush.
- When we finally dumped the piñata over, ten four-year-olds scrambled on top of each other to get the meager booty.
- Chocolate was smeared all over our white couch.
- Lollipops stuck to the new carpeting.
- Gift toys were broken.
- Our daughter suddenly found it impossible to share anything with any of her friends. Fights erupted and tears were shed.
- Three boys careened around the house screaming like wild animals.
- We were ready for the loony bin at the day's end.

The following year, we held Cherie's birthday party at the park. It lasted only an hour.

■ ■ ■

Feeling Good About Discipline
POINTS TO REMEMBER ABOUT
EXPECTATIONS AND FRUSTRATION

1. It's difficult to balance your own needs with those of your children.
2. "To avoid perversion, allow diversion."
3. What to expect from your preschooler:
   - He is gaining psychological and physical separateness from you.
   - He is egocentric.
   - He is in conflict between his self-centered desires and the needs of others.
   - His sense of conscience is just beginning to take shape.
   - He does not yet know the difference between right and wrong.
5. Preschoolers decide what is good or bad by the severity of the consequences.
6. Problems arise from clashing agendas.
7. Assess your agenda and that of your child:
   - Relax.
   - Compare sizes and ages in front of a mirror.
   - Review your own agenda.
   - Review your child's agenda.
   - Adjust your expectations so that they make sense.
8. To deal with agenda conflicts:
   - Bring along diversions.
   - Ignore minor disturbances.
   - Change your plans.
   - Use limit setting, consistent consequences, and follow-through.
9. Keep activities short and sweet.

PART TWO

Essential Elements of Disciplining with Love

CHAPTER THREE

Testing, Testing

Setting and Keeping to Your Limits with Love

IN THE PREVIOUS CHAPTER we gave you some difficult "news":

- Your preschooler is self-centered: He doesn't care about the needs and wants of others.
- He is separating from you physically and emotionally.
- He doesn't yet know wrong from right—if he can get away with something, then it must be OK!
- His agenda may be very different from yours.
- Your needs and wants are bound to come into conflict with his.

What's to be done? Loving yet firm discipline is the answer. Discipline creates structure in your child's life, especially when his demands are inappropriate. Discipline is simply a way of shaping or changing behavior so that everyone in the family can get along and work together. Remember, your preschooler needs and wants limits even if he's pushing against them with all of his might. Structure helps him to feel safe and secure.

Discipline is also a way of relating to your child. For example, if Mathew is hungry at 4:00 P.M., he may come into the kitchen whining for a cookie. One possible reaction is that you give in to his demand, even though you know you shouldn't. You can't stand his whining, and you just want to keep him quiet. The next time he wants a cookie at an inappropriate time, he knows that all he has to do is whine long enough and irritatingly enough and he'll get his way.

Another reaction (this takes a lot more energy at first, so be prepared) is for you to say, "Mathew, no cookies after 4:00 P.M. I don't want you to spoil your appetite for dinner. If you take a cookie before dinner, you get no dessert for two days. I'm going to count the cookies so that I'm sure you don't eat any more while I'm not looking."

You may also offer a choice: "You can have a carrot instead of a cookie." If he insists on the cookie, remind him, "It's a carrot or nothing. You have a choice. Just remember, if you take a cookie, you get no dessert for two days. It's up to you."

THE BASICS

The basic structure that we recommend for disciplining your preschooler in most situations boils down to four "easy" steps:

- Create the limit.
- Set a consequence if the limit is exceeded.
- Follow through on your consequence.
- Introduce the idea of choice.

These are the key elements for disciplining your preschooler. The interrelation of these four parts is essential. Limits without consequence or consequence without follow-through are harder on you and your child than no limits at all. (We will cover consistency more fully in Chapter 6). Choice helps your child to take responsibility for his actions. You might think of it as you do the running of our government. The Executive, Judicial, and Legislataive branches all interact and create checks and balances for one another. In the same way, you won't properly discipline your child unless those four elements coexist.

Your child learns from this system that he is responsible for his behavior and that his actions in the world have consequences. These are important interaction skills for a three-year-old or an eighty-three-year-old. Remember, during his formative years we may be setting our child's behavior patterns for life. The understanding of consequences and personal responsibility is crucial for our preschooler's ability to get along with others and is an integral part of his socialization skills.

Here's how the four-step system worked in the example with Mathew and the cookies:

1. *Create the limit.* "Mathew, no cookies after 4:00 P.M. I don't want you to spoil your appetite for dinner."
2. *Set the consequence.* "If you take a cookie before dinner, you get no dessert for two days."
3. *Follow through on your consequence.* "OK, Mathew, I'm going to count the cookies so that I'm sure you don't eat any more now."
4. *Introduce the idea of choice.* "It's a carrot or nothing. You have a choice. But if you sneak a cookie, you get no dessert for two days. It's up to you."

Choosing a follow-through that is feasible for you to carry out as promised is essential. For example, if you don't want to bother to keep track of the cookie tally, then you shouldn't set up that condition. Or if you can't be home everyday at 4:00

P.M. (you're certainly not going to leave work early to check on his cookie-eating habits!), you can warn your babysitter beforehand and in Mathew's presence, and ask her to report back to you on the status of the cookie jar each evening.

Follow-through also means that you should be consistent. There is nothing more confusing to your child than having a cookie rule one day and no cookie rule the next. Which one is it today? he wonders. Either I get to have cookies before dinner or I don't. Each time Mathew breaks this rule, he should lose dessert for two days. Your response should be exactly the same. Only when you follow through consistently will Mathew learn that *you mean what you say and you say what you mean.* This helps him to feel more secure and increases his feelings of trust. And after a while, it will make your life easier. He will stop testing the limits you've established. He'll believe you.

THE IMPORTANCE OF CHOICE

In their book *Assertive Discipline*, educators Lee and Marlene Canter discuss the importance of offering a choice to your child during the disciplining process. They describe a situation in which a student habitually pokes his classmates. His teacher has offered him the choice to either stop poking or sit alone. They write:

> When we provide [children] with the choice as to whether the limit-setting consequence will occur, we place responsibility where it belongs—on the [children]. They are the ones who choose to poke the other children; thus they are the ones who choose to sit by themselves. When we provide a student with a choice, we are providing him with the opportunity to learn the natural consequence of his inappropriate actions, and that he is responsible for his behavior.

A responsible child is one who has gained a valuable social skill. He feels empowered within his own life.

PUSHING THE ENVELOPE

It's only natural that your child will push at the boundaries that you have created. He may not believe you mean what you say (especially if, in the past, you were not consistent), or he may just be curious. You must be ready for this limit testing, because it is bound to occur.

Here's how that conversation will go: "I see those cookie crumbs on your lip. You had a cookie before dinner. I see that you've chosen not to have dessert tonight and tomorrow night." You don't have to be angry—just be firm and certain of the rightness of your stand. Besides, Mathew is acting normally. It's his job to test your limits at this age. You don't have to take it personally. It's not an issue of disrespect. Rather, it's a developmental stage.

Undoubtedly, Mathew will be upset at being deprived of his chocolate pudding, but you can remind him that he is responsible for the loss because he ignored the limit you had established. It was his choice. If he continues to pester you for his dessert, you can use the *broken-record approach*. Simply repeat over and over again that he has chosen no dessert because he sneaked cookies. He eventually will get the message.

If the encounter turns into a tantrum, you can follow the guidelines that we suggest below for a time-out and that we discuss more fully in Chapter 10. Whatever you do, however, stick to your limits. Otherwise, the rules will mean nothing.

This may be easier said than done. In exasperation, you may be tempted to give in. From our experience, this is the most treacherous part of parenting. None of us likes to live with our child's discomfort and displeasure. Yet when you stick to your consequence, Mathew will eventually learn that you definitely mean business. Next time he may be less likely to overstep the limit, in cookie-snatching as well as other, more serious, areas.

COMPLICATIONS

The ideal situation simply involves a limit setting-consequence-follow-through formula. But who ever said that life is easy or that children are always compliant?

Mitch had an interesting case in his psychology practice. Francine was having a problem with her four-year-old, Mara. Francine sensed that Mara never listened to her. She would tell Mara one hundred times to clean up her toys, but Mara would just go on playing. Francine was frustrated and angry, and she felt that she had no control over her daughter, that she just nagged at Mara endlessly. In some ways, Francine's feelings of powerlessness reminded here of how her own mother had treated her when she was a child. She hated repeating her mother's mistakes, yet she just didn't know what to do to change things. This was an instance where limits, consequence, and follow-through were desperately needed.

Francine was so upset by this issue that she began bringing Mara into therapy with her. In their sessions together, the opportunity arose to work with this problem. One afternoon in the office, Mara began picking at her mother's shoes. Francine didn't like it and asked Mara to stop. As you can probably guess, Mara did not comply with her mother's request.

Francine turned to Mitch with a look on her face that combined resignation, anger, and frustration. "See what I mean? She's just impossible."

Mitch asked Francine if she wanted to try a new approach. When she agreed, he modeled a more appropriate response for his client. After a bit of coaching, Francine said, "Mara, you can sit next to me, but it's not OK for you to annoy me like that—especially when I ask you to stop. If you continued to pick at my shoes, I will have to move you away from me for five minutes. It's your choice."

Mara tested the limits by fiddling with the bow on a shoe. Francine said, "Mara, you understand that you can sit next to me if you leave my shoe alone. Since you picked at it, you have chosen to have me move you over there, away from me."

"No," said Mara defiantly. "I want to stay here."

"You understood what the limits were. And now it's not up to you anymore. You've lost the privilege of sitting next to me for the next five minutes." With that, Francine got up and moved Mara over to the other side of the room, with Mitch's nodding support.

Mara screamed bloody murder at this affront. Through her cries, Francine said, "I understand that you're upset. But the rules are important for you and me. Here is a clock. When the big hand get to the 7, you can move back and sit next to me."

It was an impossible five minutes to endure. Both Francine and Mitch had visions of police cars rolling up to the building to take them away for child abuse. But it had to be done.

When the requisite time had passed, Francine allowed Mara to sit at her feet once more. But had Mara learned her lesson? Not quite. Shortly after taking up her place, she tested the limit once more. Again, the communication was repeated that she had overstepped the bounds and that she would be moved across the room. Again she responded with indignant tears. But after the second encounter with the limit, she gave up her testing. Exhausted, she laid her sweaty head on her mother's lap. Mara understood that if she wanted to sit with her mom, she was going to have to stop annoying her.

How did this translate into everday practice in Francine's household? Well, it wasn't easy.

Picking up on Mitch's cue that the consequence for Mara should be some kind of separation from her, Francine decided to send Mara to her room for overstepping a limit.

At first, Mara was very upset by this. But as time went on, Francine could hear that Mara would entertain herself by playing in her room and listening to music. That began to defeat the purpose of the consequence: It was not so terrible to be sent to one's room, after all.

In order to counteract this new wrinkle, Francine had to devise another time-out place. She put Mara on a kitchen chair and kept her under surveillance. This was not easy on Francine; it meant a big commitment on her part. But she had come to see the value of the limit setting-consequence-follow-through approach. The best way for her to be certain that the discipline was effective was to check on her daughter to make sure that she wasn't "fudging."

Eventually, Francine was able to use these kitchen-chair time-outs as a way to discipline Mara effectively. Unfortunately, it doesn't work so quickly for all children in every family.

POWER STRUGGLES

If you see that your child is repeatedly defying your limits, you may become angry and overreact. Then the conflict turns into a power struggle in which usually everyone suffers. In fact, even if you get your way and punish your child, you may win the battle but lose the war.

You explode at Mathew for sneaking cookies behind your back, and in a state of exasperation you deprive him of a month of dessert. But Mathew is smarter than you think. He can get back at you by dawdling over dinner. Using the old *spread-it-around-the-plate* trick, he turns his meal into a two-hour ordeal. "I'm not hungry," he whines. But really, he may be thinking, "Why should I eat dinner if I'm not getting dessert anyway?"

In a fit of anger, you banish him from the dinner table. Enraged, he takes it out on his room, throwing his toys around, screaming, and making a general all-around ruckus.

Meanwhile, you find your stomach tying itself into tidy little square knots. Your lasagne has gone to glue in your mouth, and you cannot swallow. You and your spouse start arguing about who is at fault.

"All I want is peace and quiet when I come home from the office. Is that too much to ask? And now, look at what I get!"

"Well, if that's how you feel, why bother coming home at all?"

It seems like more than just dinner is ruined.

When you're caught in a power struggle with your child, you should know that if you "win," if you prove that you are stronger, he will act out or get back at you in some other way. Like it or not, it's a lose-lose situation.

How to avoid this pitfall? It's essential to listen to your own communications. When you become personally involved in getting someone else to do something that you want, you are apt to run into resistance. You ego gets caught up in the fray, and you take it as an affront if your demands are disregarded.

Your child, on the other hand, doesn't like being ordered around. And, even if he complies, he will harbor resentment that can surface later. Our daughter, Cherie, at the age of four let Susan have it when she was being too bossy and controlling with her. "Stop pushing me around," Cherie exclaimed. "I'm not a meatball!"

Look at the following two statements. What is the difference between the two of them, and which one do you think is more effective?

Statement 1. "You'd better clean up your room. Do it now, or else.

Statement 2. "It's important to me that you clean up your room. I know how much it hurts if you step on your toys, and you hate to break them. Let's find a way for you to do this."

The first statement sounds like it's coming from a power-wielding bully. But actually it is a wild and empty threat.

Or else what? You know there is no answer. The second statement is much more effective. The speaker shifts the emphasis from him or herself to the child. What's implied is *It's not so much what I want. Really this has to do with you and your own safety. You need to clean you room because those are your toes and your toys.* A responsible yet cooperative spirit is encouraged.

If this still doesn't work, or if your child begins a tantrum behavior, a *time-out* may be in order.

WHEN AND HOW TO USE A TIME-OUT

On a basic level, discipline often means changing your preschooler's behavior. He is biting his sister, and you want him to stop. She is not cleaning up her room as you had asked. He is teasing you by running out into the street. The first question that you must ask yourself is if you can tolerate the behavior. Is it a danger to your child or others?

If it's simply a question of whining or hanging on to your leg at inappropriate times, sometimes merely ignoring your child's annoying behavior can make it go away. When you are not reinforcing the whining with your attention, for example, then it loses its value to your preschooler. He stops on his own.

If, on the other hand, you decide that

- the behavior is harmful to your child or others,
- your ignoring it doesn't work or isn't appropriate,
- he is testing the limits beyond your ability to tolerate it,
- he has "chosen" a more severe consequence as a result of his actions,

then a time-out may be in order. When you institute a time-our, you remove the child from the reinforcing situation.

That may simply mean separating him from contact with you for a specified period of time.

Joseph H. Brown and Carolyn S. Brown give useful guidelines on how to institute a time-out in their book *Systematic Counseling*. The following list is based on their suggestions:

1. *Use a matter-of-fact voice.* Tell your child why he is having a time-out. You can say, "You were teasing your brother, and you didn't stop when I asked you, so you've chosen to have a time-out." Scolding may reinforce the negative behavior because it is an emotionally charged form of communication. Your preschooler may perceive it as attention. Just state the facts.

2. *Use verbal and nonverbal signals.* If you perceive danger, such as seeing your child hitting his friend with a ruler, don't let him continue. Say, "Stop!"

3. *Make sure that the environment is neutral.* Francine ran into this problem with Mara. The four-year-old was only too happy to get a time-out in her room. It allowed her to play. That, of course, is not the idea of a time-out. A dull, unstimulating place, such as a kitchen chair, is appropriate. Remember when teachers used to put your misbehaving classmates (maybe even you) in the corner, facing the wall? Now you know why they did that!

4. *Monitor your child's behavior in the time-out situation.* She should be displaying appropriate behavior before you allow her to return to the family. For example, if Jessica is having a tantrum, she may need to stay in her room until the hurricane blows over. If you allow her to leave the time-out area while she's still crying, you may reinforce the tantrum behavior. She learns that if she cries loud enough and long enough, you will give in. In five to ten minutes, she should be behaving properly.

Setting limits and sticking to consequences despite our children's testing is a difficult task. Yet not only is it possible, it's essential to our peace of mind and our family's closeness and harmony. It is an expression of our love and caring for our children. For when we care enough about our kids to prevent them from hurting themselves and others, we communicate that what happens in their lives matters deeply to us.

As parents, we're even willing to put up with tantrums, if that's what it takes, for our children to understand how important it is for them to correct their behavior. And often, after the storm passes, we can sit down together as a family and talk about it. The value of family meetings is covered in our next chapter.

■ ■ ■

Feeling Good About Discipline
PROGRAM

1. The basics for discipline
   - Create the limit.
   - Set a consequence.
   - Follow through on your promise.
   - Offer choices.
2. The basics all work together.
3. Choice promotes a sense of responsibility in your child.
4. Limit testing is bound to occur. Be prepared!
5. Hold firmly to your commitment. Don't be tempted to give in if your child has a tantrum.
6. Everyone loses in power struggles. Avoid them.
7. Use time-outs to help your child cool off:
   - Use a matter-of-fact voice.
   - Use verbal and nonverbal signals.
   - Make sure the environment is neutral.
   - Monitor your child's behavior.

CHAPTER FOUR

Getting Down to Your Child's Level

The Value of Fair Family Meetings

Victorina had come into our house as a housekeeper/baby-sitter when Susan went back to work. Victorina came with excellent recommendations. She had lived with her previous family for seven years and had raised their baby from infancy. Once the child had reached school age and was relatively self-sufficient, Victorina was asked to leave, which was a terrible loss for her. But she was eager to find another baby to care for.

Since our youngest, Aimee, was about a year old, Victorina's experience seemed ideal to us. Cherie, who was four at the time, was happily ensconced in nursery school. Our work and her school hours corresponded roughly, so she did not spend that much time at home with the housekeeper without at least one of us there as well.

After about six weeks, however, trouble erupted. One Friday night we came home from a movie to find the household in an uproar. The baby was crying, and Cherie was pouting in her room. Victorina was red-faced. What had happened? We found out that Cherie had kicked the housekeeper.

We were appalled. In front of Victorina, we explained to Cherie that her behavior was not acceptable and that she should never do such a thing again to anyone. We asked her to apologize to Victorina, which she did reluctantly. "Come to us if you're unhappy. Use your words. It's never OK to hit or kick anyone," we admonished. We set up as a consequence Cherie's loss of a trip to Disneyland—something she dearly cherished—and promised to increase the severity of the consequence if she ever repeated the act.

But that wasn't the end of it. We were both very disturbed by Cherie's behavior. There had to be something else behind her act. It was not like her to kick anyone, especially an adult. We had to get to the bottom of it. The situation warranted a fair family meeting.

OUR FAIR FAMILY MEETING

The next morning, after breakfast, the three of us sat down to talk.

"How do you feel about missing Disneyland?"

"I hate Victorina," was Cherie's reply.

"What does she have to do with this?"

"If she didn't tell on me, I would still be able to go to Disneyland."

"No, Cherie," we explained. "You've got it backwards. If you hadn't kicked her, then there would be no problem. You're responsible, not Victorina, for losing the trip to Disneyland. But why were you so angry that you had to kick her anyway? What was going on with you?"

As if on cue, Cherie burst into tears. "Victorina doesn't like me. All she does is play with Aimee. Ever since Aimee came, no one loves me anymore. I wish she was never born."

Everything changed. We saw that sibling rivalry had fueled Cherie's attack on the housekeeper. This was a larger issue, but something that we could readily understand and deal with. It was clear that Cherie's misbehavior was a cry for help.

Because of her experience and loss at the termination of her previous job, Victorina had created a lovely and loving relationship with Aimee. Unfortunately, she had not been as successful in bonding with Cherie. Our assumption that Cherie's nursery school and her friends would take care of that need was incorrect.

Cherie—as all children—was sensitive to rejection, and her jealousy over her new sister was still a very tender area. Victorina's coldness toward her brought back all of her hurt feelings. It was easier and safer for Cherie to take out her anger on the housekeeper than it was for her to yell and scream at us or hit the baby. After all, we are her parents and she is still very dependent on us, and hitting her sister was too dangerous.

We felt that the best way to deal with Cherie's feelings was to reassure her that we loved her and that our love for her had not diminished since Aimee's arrival. There was room in our hearts for both children. We empathized that it must be difficult for Cherie to watch Victorina give Aimee so much attention and her very little, but we explained to Cherie that the baby-sitter was doing her job and that little children needed more ongoing care. On the other hand, we asked Victorina to play with Cherie more.

During the course of our discussion, we realized that part of the problem was our own doing. It was hard enough for Cherie to adjust to her mother going back to work, let alone having a veritable stranger in the house to care for her some portion of the day. And it was clear that she was still smarting over the loss of her position as "the one and only." Maybe we had been too cavalier about how easy the transition to the new household arrangements would be.

While we felt that we couldn't back down on the trip to Disneyland (that would be sending the wrong message to Cherie; after all, it still wasn't OK to kick the housekeeper), we tried to make amends in other ways. We each made a mental note to spend more time with Cherie. It seemed to us that she needed that. We also followed through on our discussion by asking Victorina to divide her time more equally between the two girls.

But the damage had already been done. That evening, Victorina packed her bags and left our house for good. Who could blame her?

After a week of chaotic child-care arrangements and frantic searching, we found a new housekeeper. Olga was much younger and lacked the history of loss that Victorina carried on her shoulders. She got on famously with both children.

In some ways, Cherie's acting out—as negative as it was— had a positive effect on our family. It helped us to pay attention to the family and make a correction that was necessary. Mitch has used the lesson that we all learned from this painful experience often in his work with others.

When kids misbehave in ways that are unusual for them, they are crying out for help. They need something emotionally that may not be readily apparent. It's best to approach the problem not just with limits and consequence but also with curiosity, love, and tenderness in your heart. That's often best accomplished during a fair family meeting.

WHY FAIR FAMILY MEETINGS ARE IMPORTANT

A fair family meeting is a great way to help your loved ones communicate effectively. It is a unique and brief period in time when all traditional roles are suspended. Both parent and child become equal partners in the family. Each shares his or her concerns openly and honestly. You listen to one another without distraction. You feel that your needs have been, if not resolved, at least heard. You child gains a sense of power and control within a context that is acceptable to you.

Our fair family meeting, which was called over the crisis with Victorina, proved to be very helpful. We were able to learn the truth about Cherie's feelings of anger and rejection (feelings that she had kept hidden from us or that we had been too busy to observe) because she felt safe to express herself. She knew that her feelings would be heard. We got beneath Cherie's behavior to find out what was really going on with her, and we were able (with some backhanded help from Victorina) to solve the problem for ourselves.

Fair family meetings are also important because they help your child to develop a sense of responsibility at an early age. You may confront him with questions about the motivation for his behavior. "Adam," you may ask, "help me to understand what's going on with you." You ask him to "look inside" for the answer.

Such questions not only prompt your child to assess his role in the misbehavior but also give him the freedom to express his feelings. In fact, one of the primary values of family meetings is that at an early age your child learns to put his emotions into words.

In addition, your child discovers that his words and feelings can have an effect on you. This gives him a sense of power in the family, which can only enhance his self-esteem. He learns that he is important in your eyes. What he says really matters to you. You're even willing to change situations to suit him, if his problems warrant it. When your child experiences that he has some power in the family, this positive feeling can mitigate his urge to act out and misbehave. He no longer needs to do things to get your attention. He already has it.

WHEN AND HOW TO SET UP
A FAIR FAMILY MEETING

Since the incident with Victorina, we have had many fair family meetings. Traditionally, these meetings are arranged when there is a sense that something is off balance:

- Someone's out of control.
- Someone's behavior has changed dramatically.
- Someone's needs are being ignored.
- There's a feeling that "the center isn't holding."

Or you could set up a regular meeting—say, every Friday evening—as a normal part of your family dynamics. Either parents or child can ask for a family meeting. In most cases, however, children, especially preschoolers, may be unaware of or unable to verbalize their problems, and adults often must assume the responsibility to take the initiative. The meeting can involve the whole family or just the child who is having the problem. That depends on you and your preferences. (We usually included everyone unless an issue demanded privacy.)

It may seem silly to make a discussion among family members so formal. After all, you see one another every day and talk about problems in passing. But some issues warrant special time. That's exactly what a fair family meeting is all about. Calling for a meeting means that you are all making a commitment to be involved and deal with the issues. Here are some ground rules to help you set up a successful fair family meeting:

1. *Make an appointment*. Set up the time and place. Find a quiet environment away from possible interruptions. Unplug the phone if you're apt to receive many calls. This will let your child know that you really want to talk with him and that your conversation is important enough for you to forgo

all distractions. By setting the time in advance, all family members will be sure to attend.

2. *Make it time-limited.* Specify in advance that the meeting will take about fifteen or twenty minutes (or forty-five minutes or an hour—whatever you feel comfortable with and your child's limited attention span permits). This helps to keep the meeting contained and makes it feel safer. The prospect of arguing all afternoon is not appealing to anyone.

And in truth, most issues are not resolvable in one sitting. It can be frustrating for you and your children if you go around and around without coming to some kind of agreement. The resolution of a conflict is an evolutionary process. Two or three meetings during one week may be required. Often it helps for all of you to "sleep on it." By limiting the time and setting up several meetings, you enhance the creative process.

3. *Cover a specific topic.* We had called our family meeting to deal with Cherie's feelings about Victorina. We did not throw in how we were unhappy that she wasn't feeding the dog, as she had promised, or that she left her room in a mess. Cover only one issue per meeting. Otherwise, you will only confuse your child.

A single-issue meeting helps your family to focus. The clearer you are, the clearer are the issues and the discussion and the greater is the chance for resolution. Compare it to juggling: It's easier to juggle one ball than five.

4. *Let each person have a turn.* Make sure that there is equity in the discussion. Allow enough time for each member of the family. Everyone's input and perspective are valuable and should be respected. Every person has the right to say what he wants to say, be heard, and be understood.

5. *Feel OK about leaving the problem unsolved.* It's important to remember that, although you may come to an agreement, it's not necessary for the success of your fair family meetings. There is value in each person having his or her

own say. Ultimately the resolution will come from this spirit of mutual respect and sharing.

6. *Include your child in the discussion of consequence.* If you have all decided that the misbehavior warrants some kind of consequence, ask your child what he thinks it should be. You'll be surprised to find out that sometimes kids are harsher on themselves than you would be. You might have in mind, for instance, two nights without TV, while he suggests no TV for a week. Whether or not you negotiate on the terms, your child's respect for you, himself, and the rules will be enhanced if he is included in the decision that directly affects him. He is also less apt to try to fudge on the consequence since he had a hand in setting it up himself.

7. *Prepare for the next meeting.* If you find at the end of the allotted time that further discussion is necessary, set up the time and place for the next meeting. Identify in advance the topic that you want to talk about. Most likely, this would develop from the current discussion.

COMMUNICATION SKILLS THAT CAN HELP

It's important to know that the way you communicate during your fair family meeting can be as important as calling for the meeting itself. If, for example, you are critical and put your child down constantly, the meeting will probably create more tension and unhappiness in your family than if you had not had the meeting at all. Your child may even escalate the severity of the negative behavior, which obviously is not the desired goal.

Following are twelve suggestions for communication skills that have helped us in family meetings. They will enhance how you talk to one another and may even help to increase your child's self-esteem. Of course, it may be difficult to include all of them in your family meetings at once, but you can work at incorporating them as time goes on.

1. *Sit down.* In order to have an impact on your child, you need to be on her level, both physically and emotionally. To understand why this is important in communicating with your child, try this little experiment with your spouse. Have him or her stand on a chair and carry on a conversation with you.

Now, ask yourself some questions:

- Do you feel uncomfortable with your neck craned and your back strained?
- Is it hard to communicate your feelings?
- Do you feel intimidated by your spouse's physical dominance over you?
- Now try to listen to what he or she has to say. How long can you stay in this position without feeling distressed?

You've probably forgotten what it feels like to be a child vis-à-vis the larger adult world. This exercise should rekindle in you the vulnerability that a child experiences. It's hard for your daughter to pay attention when she's down here and you're all the way up there. And if you're standing and screaming at your preschooler, she may be frightened of you and may even tune you out. You're big and tall and loud. In any case, you will not be successful in gaining what you want from her. So for the sake of family harmony, sit down.

2. *Really listen.* You may have a lot on your mind, especially if you're angry at your child for misbehaving. However, before you blast him with your point of view, it's important to listen.

Listening is a significant form of nonverbal communication. A child who is listened to feels cared about and valued. Your simple act of listening helps to increase his feelings of self-esteem. And listening is a two-way street. Both you and your child need to feel listened to in order for your fair family meeting to work. If Jeff wants to cut you off in midsentence, you can remind him that you listened to him completely when it was his turn to speak, and now you are entitled to your five minutes. Most likely, he will see the fairness in this.

3. *Make direct eye contact with your child.* The eyes have often been called the windows of the soul. Many emotions—especially love—are expressed in the eyes. Your child understands these nonverbal cues from you from earliest infancy onward. When you look into your child's eyes, you are letting him know that all of your attention is focused on him.

Of course, eye contact is also a two-way street. Greg may feel shy about meeting your eyes. You shouldn't demand that he look you in the eye, but you can say "When you look down all the time, I find it hard to know what you're feeling inside. I'm afraid I may miss what you're trying to tell me." You can even reinforce eye contact with him by saying, "The way you look me straight in the eye when we're talking makes our talk special."

4. *Ask questions in nonthreatening ways.* It's easy to find out what's happening with your child. Just ask her. But be careful how you do it.

If your question expresses criticism ("Heather, what's wrong with you? Why did you poke Samantha in the stomach? You know you're not supposed to do that!"), you may not get the answer you're looking for. The question itself is perceived as hostile, and Heather is apt to be defensive with you ("I didn't poke her." "She started it." "You always pick on me.").

If, on the other hand, you express curiosity ("Heather, I don't understand what's going on here. Help me understand why you're fighting with your sister."), you may get a more thoughtful and less defensive response. Heather may reply, "Samantha never wants to play with me." In that case, you would understand that Heather's misbehavior is a call for attention from her aloof older sister. That's a meaty subject for discussion with both daughters about their relationship.

5. *Use mirroring.* Mirroring is a way of validating your child's emotional experience. When you mirror your child's feelings, you communicate your emotional understanding of what he is saying or feeling, or what he wants. For example, if Nick doesn't want his little brother touching his trucks, you can say, "Nick, I can see that you're angry and upset at Jon. That's understandable, but its not OK to hit him."

6. *Pay attention to how you make requests.* When you ask your child to do something, make sure that you use a voice that is not emotionally charged. If you are relaxed, your child will recognize that the conversation is not a confrontation that someone has to win or lose.

In making a request, be sure to be very specific. For example, if you want Lance to clean up his room, ask him to put away his trucks, his Tinker Toys, his blocks, his socks, and his shoes. When you specify concretely what the task encompasses, you increase the likelihood that he will accomplish it.

7. *Have your child repeat to you the request.* After you have asked Lance to clean up his room in a specific manner, make sure that he understands what you have in mind by having him tell you in his own words what you expect him to do. You can say, "Lance, tell me what you're going to do."

He may reply, "I'm going to clean up my trucks, my blocks, my socks, and my shoes."

You may remind him, "Don't forget the Tinker Toys. It hurts when you step on them."

This simple interchange assures you that Lance understands the task. You are enforcing your expectation that he can accomplish the chore.

8. *Use constructive criticism.* If you've noticed that your child hasn't completed a task, as agreed, you should point it out to him. However, you can convey your criticism in a positive

way. Praise the parts of the task that your child did accomplish; otherwise, he will feel that all of his efforts were for nothing and that he'll never be good enough in your eyes. You could say, for example, "Lance, I like the way you put away your trucks, your blocks, your Tinker Toys, and your socks. But I also wanted you to put your shoes in the closet. What happened?"

Lance may admit that he just forgot. Or his response could be more complex. Make sure to listen to his reasons. He may say, "I was almost finished, and then I had to go potty. And then you called me for dinner, and I forgot."

9. *Separate the child from the act.* This is most important. In order to keep your child's self-esteem intact, it is necessary to make the distinction between the child and the things that she does of which you may disapprove. Focus on the act. If you say, "Holly, I love you, but I don't like it when you write on the wall with your crayons. It makes me angry because it's very hard to get off," you are communicating that you continue to value your child even when you find her behavior unacceptable and you are angered about it.

In contrast, if you were to say, "Holly, you're a bad girl. I left you alone for two minutes, and look at what you did. You're really naughty," you are not focusing on "the evil deed" but on the child. Holly may feel untrustworthy and sneaky. Her feelings about herself are lowered. She is now more likely to act out more aggressively and fulfill the role implied by her new label.

Separating the child from the act is also important when you're giving praise. For example, we avoided telling our daughters that they were "good girls" for following directions and behaving well. Instead, we praised our children with such statements as "I like how you're following directions" or "I'm happy that you're remembering to feed the dog every morning." Being a good girl also implies that one can be a bad girl under different circumstances. Whether your child's actions are acceptable or unacceptable, her inherent feelings of goodness about herself should remain intact.

10. *Watch* always *and* never. Words like always and never have no place in your fair family meeting. The behavior that you find irritating may be a onetime occurrence. Such global statements as "Every time I turn my back, you get into trouble" serves to lower your child's self-esteem. Stick to the issue at hand.

11. *Make* I *statements.* Parents often end up accusing and pointing a finger at their misbehaving kids ("You let the cat out again." "You got ice cream on your new dress." "You make me angry when you don't listen to me."), instead of expressing their feelings ("I don't like it when you're not careful" or "I feel angry when you leave your toys all over the living room.") *I* statements convey that you continue to accept your child even though you don't accept his undesirable behavior.

12. *Express love.* Despite the angry feelings ventilated during our fair family meetings, we always found a way to express our feelings of love toward one another. Our meetings usually ended with "huggie sandwiches"—a family love-in.

By following these guidelines, you are likely to have a successful fair family meeting. When fair family meetings conclude with hugs and kisses all around, they are a great way to express your love for one another.

■ ■ ■

Feeling Good About Discipline
FAIR FAMILY MEETING

1. Fair family meetings promote open communication and love.
2. When to set up the meeting:
   - Someone's out of control.
   - Someone's behavior has changed dramatically.
   - Someone's needs are being ignored.
   - There's a feeling that "the center doesn't hold."
   - Weekly, just to keep communication open.
3. How to set up the meeting:
   - Make an appointment.
   - Limit the time.
   - Cover a specific topic.
   - Let each person have his turn.
   - Let it be OK to leave a problem unresolved.
   - Include your child in the discussion of the consequences.
   - Prepare for the next meeting.
4. Communications tools that help:
   - Sit down.
   - Really listen.
   - Make eye contact.
   - Ask questions in nonthreatening ways.
   - Use mirroring.
   - Pay attention to how you make requests.
   - Have your child repeat the request.
   - Use constructive criticism.
   - Separate the child from the act.
   - Watch *always* and *never*.
   - Make *I* statements.
   - Express love.

CHAPTER FIVE

Let the Consequence Fit the Crime

MOST PARENTS IMPULSIVELY hand down an immediate punishment when their child misbehaves. Punishment is the imposition of your will on your child. A consequence, on the other hand, grows logically out of the misbehavior. Consequences are distinct from punishments. Interestingly enough, children are quick to recognize the difference between the two. They respond to logical consequence, and they fight back when punished.

Indeed, often parents later regret punishments made in the heat of anger. We realize after the fact that we overreacted, and we recognize our unreasonableness and feel guilty. Impulsive reactions, however, are normal. After all, we are parents but we are also human. Sometimes these reactions come from built-up frustration—sort of the "kick the cat" syndrome—that may not relate to the child.

THE FORK DROP

This situation happened to Mitch. Before he became a psychologist, he was an assistant principal at Montebello Intermediate School (filled with 1,500 preadolescents!) in East Los Angeles, a relatively high-crime area that is well known for its gang activity. His was an extraordinarily stressful job. After a full day of managing potential gang warfare, family violence, runaways, and firecrackers in the toilet, Mitch had to find his way home across 20 miles of congested freeway traffic. Often the trip took an hour or more of stop-and-go driving. By the third year at the job, the stress from this routine began to take its toll on Mitch. Unfortunately, the fallout would affect the entire family.

When Mitch arrived at the doorstep after work, he was exhausted and grouchy. Susan, ever the devoted wife, had dinner hot and ready to serve. But dinnertime had become an unpleasant moment. Mitch was too stressed to bear any noise at the table. The usual banter and conversation among the children had to be silenced. If one of the girls so much as dropped a fork, Mitch would start in his chair as if a gun had gone off next to his ear. (Later we recognized that his reaction was similar to the kind of posttraumatic stress that soldiers experience after combat.) Then he would explode in a rage and send the offending party to her room.

It didn't take Susan long to decide the family needed a meeting to discuss this behavior (see Chapter 4). The punishment was not fitting the offense. After all, how "bad" was it to drop a fork? Did it deserve banishment from the family? We all agreed that something was seriously wrong.

As a result of our discussion, we concluded that the stress of Mitch's job was interfering with his ability to relate to his family and with our family's closeness. He was just too overwrought to have the patience that was required to deal with two boisterous preschoolers. He couldn't tolerate any noise.

The obvious solution was for Mitch to quit his job. But this was not practical at that point. Other solutions were necessary. Sometimes in life we have to deal with certain unfortunate givens and reach a "good enough" solution. We decided that since Mitch couldn't leave his job and yet couldn't handle being with us when he walked in the door, we could perhaps alter our behavior when he came home. We thought it best that he *shouldn't have to* be with us from the moment he walked in the door. He needed a cooling-off period so that he could decompress.

That meant that Mitch would come in, say "Hi," and then go straight to the bedroom to relax or nap for about twenty minutes. This took a lot of discipline on everyone's part. We wouldn't stop him to tell him about our day. We wouldn't show him our new drawing or ask him to fix our Big Wheels. We wouldn't wave under his nose the letter that came from the IRS. This was his time, and we all knew how much he needed it and that it was to everyone's benefit to respect it.

Our plan worked quite well. Mitch's quiet time created a buffer between his work life and family life. Once he got to the table, he was calmer and more capable of dealing with the family activities around dinnertime.

The kids felt better about their father, and he felt better about himself and them. In fact, the stress of that job ultimately led Mitch to change professions. He left school administration for clinical psychology. And as for future dropped forks? That had a way of working itself out. Since there was no crime, there was no punishment.

It was sad that Mitch had taken his frustration out on our children. Yet, it's not an unusual thing for parents to do. Fortunately, we recognized the problem and did what we could to alleviate it before it did too much damage to us all.

The dropped-fork incident in our family should help to alert you to situations in which you are taking out your frustrations inappropriately on your child. But what if she really misbehaves? Suppose she pours salt into the sugar bowl, unrolls the toilet paper and tries to flush it down the toilet, or practices writing the alphabet on your newly hung dining room wallpaper? You want to wring her neck. You know that the act requires an appropriate consequence. What should you do? How do you choose a consequence that fits?

NATURAL CONSEQUENCE: LEARNING THE HARD WAY

There are several forms of appropriate consequences. The simplest is a natural consequence. A natural consequence of your child's act is a straightforward result of something that he has done. Sometimes, you can think of natural consequences as learning the hard way. A few examples follow:

- If Steven pulls the dog's tail, he may get bitten.
- If he touches the hot stove, he will burn his hand.
- If he runs across the street, he may get hit by a car.
- If he spits in his older brother's hair, he may have a fight and an irate mother on his hands.
- If he eats too many sweets, he may feel sick.

Obviously, you don't want to encounter certain natural consequences, such as being hit by a car. Your aim in disciplining your preschooler is to shield him from hurting himself and others. And many natural consequences are clearly dangerous. Most likely you will want to stop your child before he gets to experience the painful lesson.

Although many natural consequences can be harmful, there are some that are helpful in disciplining your preschooler. In his book *Children: The Challenge*, psychologist Rudolph Dreikurs shows how natural consequences can be useful when disciplining your child. The following is an incident from Mitch's practice that illustrates Dreikurs' ideas:

At four years old, Jennifer is underweight and has a low resistance to catching a cold. Her parents worry about this. They are certain that her poor appetite is at fault. They have a personal investment in her eating. "If only she would eat more, she would stay healthier and look as robust as the other kids," they lament.

Witness a typical scene at mealtime: Jennifer eats the first few bits of lunch hungrily and drinks a bit of milk. But as the conversation between her parents becomes more animated, she starts pushing her food around the plate. She swings her legs back and forth and makes crisscross fork patterns in her mashed potatoes. Clearly, her mind is not on her lunch.

"Come on, sweetie pie," coaxes her dad, lovingly. "Don't you want your lunch?"

Jennifer gives him a big smile and pops a piece of chicken into her mouth. She doesn't chew it, however. She just holds it there. Her parents once again engage in conversation. Jennifer's jaws move once or twice.

"Go ahead. Chew it up," urges her mom, interrupting the conversation. "You want to grow up to be a big girl, don't you?"

Jennifer gives her parents what they crave for the moment.

Dad compliments her. "That-a-girl. I knew you could do it."

But as soon as Jennifer's parents resume speaking to each other, she stops eating. In fact, the whole drawn-out affair is one of this four-year-old's parents encouraging her to do what should come naturally.

The truth is Jennifer doesn't necessarily have a poor appetite, but she has learned that if she doesn't eat, her parents will stop what they are doing and attend to her exclusively. What a great way for her to get their undivided attention.

What can Jennifer's parents do differently to ensure that their daughter eats without all the cheerleading? Here is where a natural consequence can be used as a teaching device.

1. The easiest way for Jennifer to learn how to eat is for her parents to *let her eat*. If she refuses to eat, her parents should not get angry and should not remind her to do what is expected.

2. When everyone else is finished, they can remove her plate from the table so that Jennifer will discover for herself the natural consequence of not eating: She will get hungry later.

3. At the next meal (and *not before*) food is offered again.

4. If Jennifer still dawdles, her parents should refrain from saying anything and not get angry. (We know this takes a lot of discipline on the parents' part, but it can be achieved.) If she refuses to eat, remove the meal casually. What's implied is "If you want to eat, here is the food. If you don't eat, I have to assume that you're not hungry." They do not threaten punishment or bribe her with chocolate ice cream.

5. An hour later, Jennifer may complain that she's hungry. She may even beg for milk and cookies. Her mother can reply, "I'm sorry that you're so hungry. Dinner will be at six. It's too bad that you have to wait so long."

This approach may seem harsh. Yet think about it. As adults, we realize that all of our actions bear consequences. If we forget to make a deposit in our checking account, our checks will bounce. We will be charged outrageous fees, and our creditors may get angry. In the future, we will be more careful about our bank balances.

Jennifer needs to learn that her actions have consequences, too. So regardless of how pitiable her complaints may be, her mother should allow her to be hungry for the moment. Hunger is a natural consequence of not eating. Jennifer will surely eat the next meal.

If parents use a natural consequence as a threat or impose it in anger, however, the consequence stops being a natural consequence and becomes a punishment. For example, if after the second meal Jennifer's father becomes exasperated when she refuses to eat, he may say, "OK, don't eat lunch. But you'll see. You'll get hungry. And remember. Nothing until dinner." Jennifer will perceive this as a punishment since she is being threatened with hunger. The consequence seems to be inflicted by an adult rather than being the natural outgrowth of her not eating.

Natural consequences can't be used for all of your disciplining needs. But they are helpful in some situations. When else can you employ a natural consequence?

1. Jonathan is notorious for being late for nursery school, making you frenzied and almost late for work every morning. He refuses to get dressed on time. The natural consequence? You bring him to school in his pajamas and slippers. Or you arrange with your sympathetic boss for the possibility that you will arrive late for work one week, and you take Jonathan to school when he's ready. He will have to face the peer pressure from his friends and the disapproval of his teacher. (This may require the teacher's cooperation as well.)

2. Annie is always losing toys and special transitional objects, such as articles of clothing, stuffed animals, or pieces of diaper or blankets that children get attached to as a way of comforting themselves—the famous security blanket. Finally, one day she leaves her favorite "blankie" at nursery school and remembers the loss only at bedtime. She may cry and carry on at night, refusing to sleep without her cherished friend.

Rather than calling up the school director and setting up a midnight rendezvous to retrieve the shredded blanket, you put up with her discomfort, reminding her that she needs to be more careful with things that are important to her. You can be sure that she will not forsake her blankie at school again and that she may even become more careful about her other possessions.

3. Michael continues to resist toilet training but refuses to wear a diaper, since he wants to be "a big boy." If he wets his pants at nursery school, the peer pressure and his own dis-

comfort may help him to see the benefits of using the facilities. (To all of our readers who are still wringing their hands over wet training pants, rest assured that as far as we know, no senator or congressional representative went to Capitol Hill in diapers. Everyone gets the hang of it, eventually.)

4. Marjorie refuses to go to sleep on time. She claims that she wants to stay up all night long. Rather than getting into a power struggle with her at bedtime, Marjorie's parents accede to her wishes. The first night she makes it to midnight. She is triumphant at her glorious feat. The second night she succumbs to sleepiness by 10:00 P.M. The third night, after having spent the day being ultracrabby, she nods out in front of the TV at 8:00 P.M. By the fourth night, her 7:30 bedtime is observed without a fuss. And there are no future problems.

5. Tommy wants to show off what a big boy he is. He brings five pennies to the beach. He throws the pennies over his shoulder to prove that he can find them in the sand. This works the first two times. But the third time, to make it even more challenging, he closes his eyes and twirls himself around while he tosses the coins. Tommy comes home from the beach a little poorer but wiser.

6. Debbie insists on going out to play in the snow without wearing her jacket. She claims she's too hot. She hates that old jacket anyway and has a tantrum when her father tries to get it on her. Finally, he says, "OK. See if you like the snow with no jacket on to keep you warm." He stands on the porch and watches her. She plays for about three minutes before coming back to him, her freezing hands jammed into her jeans pockets. "I cooled off. I'll get my coat now," she says meekly.

LOGICAL CONSEQUENCE: OF COURSE!

Sometimes natural consequences prove too dangerous or, conversely, don't provide a powerful enough deterrent. You may create a logical consequence that is based on the natural consequence if you set up the limit in advance. Logical consequences are created by parents or parents in conjunction with their children. Often the interested parties negotiate the logical consequence.

Logical consequences are in some way related to the misbehavior. In Chapter 3, Mathew's parents deprived him of dessert for two days because he ate cookies before dinner. That's a logical consequence. Taking away TV privileges for a week is not a logical consequence of sneaking cookies, since watching television is not connected to the behavior of sneaking cookies in any way.

Some examples of ways to state your limit and its logical consequence are as follows:

- "Be gentle with Spot, or you won't be able to play with him. I'll put him out in the yard until you're ready to be nice to him."
- "If you step off the curb without holding my hand, then you'll have to come in. I won't let you play outside."
- "If you boys can't get along with each other, I'll separate you."
- "You may have one piece of candy after dinner. If you take more, you'll not be allowed any for two days."

From these logical consequences, children learn that dogs are to be treated with respect, the streets are only for cars and grownups, big brothers don't enjoy being insulted and may seek revenge, and there is a limit to how much sugar one's body can tolerate—and they learn these things without having to suffer the natural consequences of their actions.

You can also create a logical consequence that is "pure"— that is, not based on the natural consequence.

- "If you don't put your toys away now, I will put them away for you, and you won't have them for a week."

- ■ "If you turn on the cartoons when you're supposed to be watching *Sesame Street*, you'll lose TV privileges tomorrow."
- ■ "If you splash water all over the bathroom with your boat, I won't let you have it in the tub tomorrow."
- ■ "If you won't talk to me in a normal voice and continue screaming, you'll have to take a five-minute time-out."

Remember to follow through on the consequence you've created when the limit is tested. This is most important. You will learn in the next chapter that if you are inconsistent in enforcing the consequence, you child's behavior will deteriorate, not improve.

To ensure that you are consistent in enforcing the consequence, *carefully choose a logical consequence that is realistic* within the time limit that you've specified. For example, if you have told Sean that there will be no TV for two days, you must be in a position to monitor TV-watching behavior in order for him to know that you mean business. If you're out and forget to tell the baby-sitter, this consequence is meaningless. In addition, if there is no room in the house where Sean can reasonably stay while the other household members are watching TV, then you have chosen an unrealistic consequence. Choose carefully. An unrealistic consequence can lead to ineffective disciplining.

WHEN YOU'VE MADE A MISTAKE

Although the ideal is to create safe limits and consequences that guide our children's growth and development, sometimes our reactions to their misbehavior comes from issues that have gone unresolved in our own lives.

1. *Situations and responses that we encountered as children may be repeating in our offspring.* Suppose that you were a whiny

child who was frequently punished for your whininess. Now your son is whiny, as well.

2. *If we are unaware of the connections, we may respond in much the same way that our parents did.* When you yell at David to stop whining, he whines back at you, "I'm not whining," in a familiar and irritating tone. You grab him by the shoulders and shake him in an unconscious show of anger and frustration. This is exactly how your parents had dealt with your whining.

3. *We may be angered to see in our kids parts of our own vulnerability or struggles that we don't like or cannot accept in ourselves.* David's feeling of neediness and your perception that he's never satisfied trigger your own ancient history. You hated those feelings in yourself, and you hate even more seeing them in your child. You thought you were over that already.

It's hard to admit that you've acted impulsively and badly, especially if you feel guilty about it. Such a situation happened to Susan, and more than twenty years after it occurred, she still bears the weight of it.

IN AND OUT OF THE TRASH CAN

Cherie was never a great eater. It was one of her ways of feeling her own power, given that she was blessed with a somewhat controlling and protective mother. Just like Jennifer, her dawdling was also a great means of gaining attention during mealtime.

One day at lunch, Susan prepared Cherie's sandwich and walked out for a few minutes. When she returned, the plate was clean. Now, this was unheard of. Usually it took twenty minutes for Cherie to consume what other kids ate in ten. "What happened to your tuna sandwich?" Susan asked.

"I ate it," replied Cherie gaily. "Can I have dessert now?"

"Sure," Susan said, feeling uneasy. "But how did you finish it so fast?"

"I guess I was hungry," Cherie answered over her shoulder as she picked up her chocolate-chip cookie and ran out of the kitchen.

Susan was suspicious. Cherie had been too glib. Susan had a hunch. Investigating the kitchen trash can then and there, sure enough, she discovered a half-eaten sandwich fairly well hidden in a paper towel. Her response was instant and visceral. She found this intolerable. She was enraged.

"Cherie, come here this instant," she cried.

Cherie ran in, trembling at the sound of her mother's angry voice.

"What do you see here?"

"It's my sandwich," the four-year-old gulped as she peered into the can at the evidence of her dastardly deed.

"What's it doing here?"

"I don't know," she began to cry. "I couldn't eat any more. I was full. So I just threw it away."

"I want you to take it out of the trash and eat it! You're never to do that again."

Cherie dutifully followed her mother's orders, and she probably never threw her lunch away at home again. Or if she did, her methods were most likely much more effective.

But what about Susan? When she cooled off enough to think about it, she felt tormented by her outburst. She was afraid that she had abused her child and caused her irreparable harm. She felt anguished at having lost control over a petty infraction. After all, what's the value of a half-eaten tuna sandwich compared with a child's love and self-esteem? She felt ashamed.

On deeper reflection, Susan realized that Cherie's untoward act brought to mind a scene from her own childhood, along with years of conflict and pain. Mealtime was always problematic at her home, where both she and her sister were balky eaters. Susan recalled one afternoon when she tried to get rid of her Kaiser-roll sandwich by flushing it down the toilet. Unfortunately, the roll was light enough to float. As her lunch twirled slowly around and around the bowl, unable to make the final plunge, she was mortified that she would be discovered in her evil deed. Susan hated to see her own child caught in the same trap, playing the games of chance. Besides, how else would she have even thought to check the trash?

Once Susan realized where the rage had come from, she could put the whole incident in proper perspective. She apologized to Cherie for making her punishment so unreasonable, and she promised to give her smaller sandwiches in the future. But she couldn't take back her words or undo what she had done. To this day she still feels guilty about that tuna sandwich.

WHAT WOULD HAVE BEEN A BETTER RESPONSE?

If you've already meted out the unreasonable consequence, as in the case of the trashed lunch, an apology to your child is the best thing you can do. If, on the other hand, you've "promised" the consequence but have not yet acted on it, you have several options to rectify the situation:

1. *Apologize.* You can say, "I'm sorry. I thought it over, and I realize that I made a mistake," which will help get the ball rolling. Parents can make mistakes and come back to make amends. You are not being weak by admitting to your own misjudgments. Your child will see you as having taken responsibility for your own mistake. Remember, however, that your apology is meaningless without a change in your actions. You are modeling an appropriate behavior. This is effective parenting.

2. *Give yourself time to think it over.* Separate yourself from your child and the incident, so you can think logically. Sleep on it if you have the time. Discipline becomes more creative and fun when you come up with useful and meaningful consequences.

3. *Reevaluate the consequence.* You can say, "There has to be a consequence for what you did, but not the one I first told you." In our family's case, Susan could have deprived Cherie of dessert for several days for her act, or she could have had her daughter send a portion of her small weekly allowance to UNICEF or another food-relief fund. The first alternative would have taught Cherie that if she misbehaves she loses out; the second would have included that lesson but would also have impressed on her the fact that her life was relatively privileged. The world's resources are not so easily dispensed with.

4. *Include your child in the activity of the consequence.* In that way, he doesn't feel that the consequence is just dropped on him from you the authority. If, for example, Seth broke your neighbor's window with his ball, both you and he need to apologize to the neighbor and offer to pay for the damages. While Seth certainly couldn't cover the cost of replacing the window, he may contribute from his allowance. Most certainly he will be more careful how he throws the ball the next time out.

HOW DO YOU KNOW WHEN THE CONSEQUENCE FITS THE CRIME?

Unfortunately, child abuse aside, there are not a lot of rules about appropriate consequences. Most important, you and your child have to be able to live with yourselves and the consequences you choose. You must trust your inner feelings concerning when it's right and when it's wrong. Yet the more original and creative the solution, the more willingly your child will go along with it, the more fun discipline can become, and the better you will feel about your role as a parent.

■ ■ ■

Feeling Good About Discipline
CONSEQUENCES

1. Sometimes parents overreact because of problems in their own lives—current or past.
2. Natural consequences:
   - Use them when they are safe.
   - Don't threaten your child with natural consequences.
3. Logical consequences are related to misbehavior.
4. If you have overreacted:
   - Apologize and alter your actions.
   - Give yourself time to think it over.
   - Reevaluate the consequences.
   - Include your child in the activity of the consequence.

CHAPTER SIX

Toys in the Trash

Consistency and
Follow-Through

ROOM CLEANUP was no one's favorite time at our house. It was Susan's policy that the kids could drag out as many toys and create as much chaos in their room as they wanted ("dirty" play, like painting or claywork, were done outside or in the kitchen, where spills did not leave permanent mementos in the carpeting), so long as they put away their toys every evening before bedtime. She felt this was a fair rule, since it allowed the children full rein in using imaginative exploration and play while it taught them responsibility for taking care of their possessions.

And indeed, it was successful in achieving the first goal. Barbie cities, furnished with every conceivable amenity, were set up across half the floor space. Bristle-block and Lego buildings abounded. Medieval castles, complete with king, queen, coach, horses, and entourage, sprang up next to the toy box. On any given day, crayons, paper, Tinker Toys, dolls in their doll carriages, cotton balls, Noah's ark with animals, puzzle pieces, roller skates, jacks, marbles, beads for stringing, Candy Land game cards, records, books, furry koala bears, and mechanical barking dogs, big and small, were strewn about. This excluded, of course, socks, shoes, T-shirts, underwear, and other clothes.

The children had no trouble with the first half of the equation. They became experts at making a mess when they played. It was all part of the fun. But the second half of the rule became torture. They hated to clean up.

As you can imagine, this attitude was the source of many conflicts and power struggles in our family. On the one hand, Susan was loath to restrict the children's play. She knew that all-out "pretend" was great for their intellectual, emotional, and creative development. After all, play is a child's work. On the other hand, the girls simply would not cooperate in the way that she wanted. When she came to the door and said, "OK, cleanup time," her request was met with an endless litany of whining:

"Do I have to?"

"Can't we play for ten more minutes?"

"We just finished setting up. We don't want to put it away!"

"Can I do it while I'm watching Sesame Street?"

Worse yet, at other times her requests were just ignored.

It was not a pretty scene. Susan was feeling exasperated. Finally, she enlisted Mitch's help. After hearing her out, he reminded her that she was not using consequences consistently:

- Sometimes she gave in to the children's disinterest and left the room dirty.
- Sometimes she blew her stack.
- Sometimes she made a game of cleaning up.
- Sometimes she wheedled and cajoled.
- Sometimes she cleaned up with them.
- Sometimes she got tired of arguing and threw up her hands and cleaned the room herself. It was easier than the struggle, she told herself.

But what did this tell the children?

- "Mom doesn't always mean what she says."
- "We can manipulate her."
- "What a great way to get attention!"
- "Mom is not predictable. Sometimes she gets angry, and sometimes she doesn't—at the very same thing."

And worst of all:

- "If we hold out long enough, she will clean the room for us, so why should we do it?"

Simply yelling or doing the cleaning for the kids was not effective in getting them to do it for themselves. So together we worked out a plan that we presented to the children during a family meeting:

"You know how we're always fighting about your room," Susan said. "Well from now on, Daddy and I have a new rule. When I ask you to put away your toys, I expect you to do it. You will have ten minutes by the clock. After ten minutes, if you haven't cleaned up all the toys on the floor, you will choose to have us put in this bag anything that hasn't been put away. Your toys will stay there for a week, but if you have to do this again, we will throw them away. We will warn you two minutes before your time is up. It's your choice. Clean up, or lose your toys for a week."

This was hard for the kids to believe. After all, Susan had not followed through consistently on cleanup before. Why should she now? But they agreed that they understood.

The next day, when playtime was over, Susan and Mitch used their new routine. "OK, cleanup time," reminding the girls that they had ten minutes to accomplish the task. They showed them where the hands would be on the clock when they would return to check.

This did not work like a charm. As we've already discussed in Chapter 3, children are bound to test the limits that you create. Besides, our daughters had no precedent. We had not followed through consistently before; why should things be different now? So, it was playtime as usual for the next eight minutes.

The sounds of children busily cleaning up were not emanating from the room. Susan began to fume. She had to restrain herself from bursting in on them and yelling that they were not paying attention to the cleanup rule. She couldn't believe that they would let her put away their beloved toys for a week. She wanted to warn them that they were endangering their toy supply, but she kept silent.

At two minutes before the appointed moment, Mitch appeared at the door to sound a warning. "Two minutes," he said, waving a large grocery shopping bag at them. "Whatever is left on the floor goes in here and out to our secret hiding place."

Now they looked up in horror. It was true! He would do it. They shrieked and jumped up from their game. They had to clean up. There was no alternative. As they scurried madly around the room, their time ran out. Mitch came in and began to load up the bag with the toys on the floor while the kids wailed. Aimee dove for her favorite blankie and saved it by throwing it on the bed. Cherie retrieved her picture books and crayons. Panic and mayhem prevailed, but in truth, Mitch's booty did not include much of value.

"By not cleaning up your room as we asked," Mitch reiterated as he was leaving them to their own devices, "you have chosen to have me put away the toys for a week. I hope we won't have to throw them away next time."

We didn't!

FOLLOW-THROUGHS, NOT THREATS

What's the difference between a threat and a follow-through? According to a great book, *Assertive Discipline* by Lee Canter with Marlene Canter, written for teachers but whose principles can also be applied to long-suffering parents,

> Assertive teachers [and parents] "promise" rather than threaten to follow through on their verbal requests. A "promise" is a vow of affirmative action. A "threat" is a statement or expression of intention to hurt or punish. Assertive teachers [and parents] "promise" to follow through, because they are aware that providing needed limit-setting consequences is an affirmative action which benefits the [child].

When you set up a limit, you are promising to follow through with the consequence. And, as we explained in the previous chapter, it's really important to set up the consequence that you can live with.

Such idle threats as, "You'd better be nice to your brother, or else," "If you make your clothes dirty, you're going to get it," or "I'm going to kill you if you don't get over here this instant," are impossible to follow through on. Your child learns this quickly and pays no attention to these types of statements.

One of the hidden stumbling blocks to effective discipline is our fear that our kids will feel resentment about our actions if we follow through on them. Many parents hope that if they use the right threat, it will frighten their kids into submission, and they won't have to resort to the consequence.

This is a painful method, however. It reminds us of how often we had been threatened by adults when we were children. And it emphasizes fear, not choice and consistent consequence. On the other hand, promising to follow through on a consequence and then doing it promptly as you promised teaches your child that you mean business.

Nevertheless, sometimes we set up consequences that we are reluctant to follow through on. This was true in our case. We did not want to throw away our children's toys, since we had spent our hard-earned money to buy them, and we were not in the habit of discarding perfectly good possessions. Our kids were well aware of this. Yet toy-dumping was a logical consequence of the girls' inaction. We had promised the consequence, and we were bound to fulfill it. In the process, we taught our kids several lessons:

- "Cleaning the room must be really important for Mommy and Daddy. They were willing to throw away our toys because of it."
- "If you don't take care of your things, you don't get to use them."
- "Mommy and Daddy mean what they say and say what they mean."

Susan also learned a thing or two. Most important, she learned how to get the kids to do what was expected of them without her having to scream and nag.

In truth, we had hoped that the specter of trashing the toys would be sufficient to get the girls moving. Unfortunately, it wasn't. We had to made good our word if we were to maintain any semblance of order in the household. You have to be ready to carry out the consequence in order for it to have any meaning. This means you must promise a consequence that you can carry out.

YOU'RE MEAN! THE CONSISTENCY DILEMMA

When we made good on a promised consequence, our children often express their displeasure. They may not like what you're doing and may say, "You're mean" or "I hate you." And, they may say it as if they really mean it. Consistency in follow-through is the most difficult part of being a parent. We all want to feel that our kids love us, and we do want to please them and make them happy. However, inherent in that wish are the seeds of difficulty.

If your kids say that they hate you or that you're mean, it hurts. Their attitude is not going to make you feel better about sticking to your commitment to limits and consequences. But stick to it you must. It's impossible to be liked by everyone all of the time. After all, you don't always like what your kids do. They don't always have to like what you do, either. That's OK.

Children are entitled to want what they want. But that doesn't mean that you have to give in to what they want. After all, your preschooler, sweet and lovable as he is, is still only a child. He is not all-knowledgeable about the appropriate approach to child-rearing. And, if he manages to manipulate you into abandoning your promised consequence, you—and he—may be worse off than if you had not created the limit in the first place.

THE PERILS OF INTERMITTENT REINFORCEMENT

As a part of their research on how animals and people respond to different kinds of stimulation, over the years behavioral scientists have carried out many experiments to see how animals react when rewarded or denied a treat.

A typical experiment involves a pigeon, which learns to peck at a lever in its cage. On every tenth peck, the pigeon is rewarded with a pellet of food. This is consistent and predictable reinforcement. Now the scientist changes the experiment so that the pigeon is rewarded the food randomly. That means sometimes it pecks twice, and a pellet rolls out. Sometimes it has to peck fifteen times. There is no way for the pigeon to predict how many pecks it's going to take to secure the prize. In scientific circles, this is called an intermittent-reinforcement schedule.

What do you suppose happens as a result of intermittent reinforcement? Is the pigeon likely to give up in frustration because it never knows when the pellet will come? Well, in reality, just the opposite occurs. Since the pigeon can't predict how many pecks it's going to take to gain its piece of food, it increases its pecking rate dramatically. Scientists would say that intermittent reinforcement is highly reinforcing.

How do such experiments translate into parenting skills that will help you in disciplining your preschooler? In truth, these experiments are most instructive. When parents complain that disciplining techniques just don't work, it's because they have fallen victim to the intermittent-reinforcement schedules.

For example, when Susan was alternately ignoring and punishing our children for the same misdeed, she sent them mixed messages. Each time she was inconsistent, she recreated the pigeon's reinforcement schedule. The girls figured eventually she would give up her tirade and do the work for them. They just had to wait long enough for it to happen. Kids will hold out longer and longer and test you more and more before they act in a way that you consider appropriate. They want to see if you really mean it this time.

One of Mitch's clients fell into this same trap. Four-year-old Justin was continually having a problem falling asleep. He wouldn't stay in his bed because he just felt he was missing out on something special when his parents spent time together without him in the evening. He asked for milk. He asked for water. He wanted another bedtime story. And when all else failed, he cried.

Mitch suggested to Justin's parents that they needed to create a systematic pattern at bedtime. They all agreed that the best approach was to put Justin to bed firmly, knowing that all his bodily needs had been met, and then to ignore his requests and his tears.

The following week, the family returned to Mitch's office frustrated and in despair. The plan hadn't worked. Yes, they had followed the directions. But no matter what they did, Justin still didn't stop crying at bedtime.

Mitch explored further. Were they absolutely consistent in their follow-through? Yes, most of the time they could ignore Justin's crying, but on two occasions they couldn't stand it anymore. They took him out of his bed and brought him into theirs.

No wonder the crying kept up. This was an intermittent-reinforcement schedule. Justin did not know how much crying it was going to take before his parents finally gave in and came to rescue him from his bed. So he kept on crying. He could have gone on all night if exhaustion hadn't interceded.

CREATING CONSISTENCY IN FOLLOW-THROUGH

We're not saying it's easy to let your child "cry it out." God knows we've suffered with that ourselves. In the morning we would awaken feeling as if we had been chewed up and spat out. Our jaws were tight and our muscles sore from having been tense all night. No, it's not easy, but sometimes it's necessary.

And to make matters worse, any systematic program of discipline that you institute in your home will elicit your child's complaints. You may feel like an ogre. You may break out in a cold sweat when your preschooler carries on and on. You may worry about what the neighbors will think and hide your face when you come and go from your home.

But the truth is that by creating a consistent system of follow-through in your family, you will be building trust, closeness, and love. Your children will feel cared for and cared about. They will know exactly where you stand and what to expect from you. They learn that they can depend on you. All of it works together to make disciplining easier as time goes on.

In disciplining your preschooler, you are most often trying to change his behavior, from not cleaning up his room to cleaning up his room, from not going to bed on time to keeping to a bedtime schedule, and from interrupting your conversation with other adults to leaving you in peace. The following are some suggestions to help you maintain consistency in follow-through as you make these changes:

1. *Start with small increments.* Most people have a tendency to want a problem solved immediately and all at once. In fact, they want it solved as soon as it has been identified. This is not realistic. If you want to change your preschooler's behavior, it's best to work on a small piece of it at a time. If he starts picking up his toys but forgets his clothes, praise his attempt and add just one suggestion for change. You can say, "It's great that you're cleaning up your toys. Once you put away your shoes, your room will look much neater."

In Chapter 7 we will explore how you can use positive reinforcement to help achieve your disciplining goals. You will feel successful and ready to tackle step two after you have mastered step one.

2. *If you are married, work as a husband-and-wife team.* When both of you are raising your children together, it's most important that you maintain a consistent approach with each other. Discuss the problem behavior and agree on the consequence before you speak to your child. There should be no chinks in the armor. If there are, your preschooler is sure to find them. We discuss how you can present a united front in Chapter 9.

3. *Use lots of praise.* Even if your child falls short of your expectations, praise his efforts. This will give him the impetus to try harder the next time. You can say, "Great! You almost

did it." If you are endlessly critical, your child may give up. He may feel that he'll never meet your expectations. So why bother? Or he may turn the criticism against himself and believe that he'll never be good enough. Neither of these is a desirable reaction.

4. *Set up the consequence as a choice.* The option may be the devil or the deep blue sea for your preschooler, but choice helps him to take responsibility for his action. Choice also shifts the consequences from your shoulders to his. If you say, for example, "Brian, you can choose to eat cookies now or no dessert for two days," your son will see the alternatives. If he tests the limit, you can deprive him of his dessert but remind him that this outcome was his choice. He made the decision to raid the cookie jar, knowing full well what the consequence would be.

5. *Use a consequence routinely when an infraction occurs.* If you make up your mind to carry out a consequence, it must be done matter-of-factly each time a misbehavior occurs. Otherwise, your child's behavior will get worse, not better.

6. Give yourself enough time. Whenever you plan to change behavior, make sure to allow enough time for your child to get the idea that you mean business. This may depend on how long your pattern of intermittent reinforcement has been in place. The longer you have been inconsistent, the more you are going to be tested. Be strong and be patient.

THE LONG-TERM RESULTS ARE WORTH IT

Why is it so important to discipline the preschooler with consistent follow-through? Although it may seem impossible to you at the moment, preschoolers do grow up. They become school-age children, preadolescents, and (God help us) teenagers all too soon. Take it from us, we've been down that road already. If you and your child have not worked out discipline issues during early childhood, it's much more difficult to institute change later on. On the other hand, if you finally get your discipline motor in gear, it makes parenting all the easier as your kids become more and more independent.

An incident with Aimee when she was fifteen years old made this point clear. Susan and Aimee had worked out a routine so that Aimee could get to the beach herself during the summer. Susan dropped Aimee off at the bus stop on her way to work and picked her up from the bus stop on her way home at 5:00 P.M.

This was all well and good until one day when Aimee didn't arrive at the appointed place until 5:20 P.M. Susan was tired and grouchy. She had to go home to make dinner. She was not too pleased when Aimee dragged herself off the bus twenty minutes late. Yes, there was traffic and there was congestion—we live in Los Angeles, after all. Susan let it go with a plea to be punctual the next time.

Unfortunately, the next time Aimee was late again. There had been an accident, and the buses wouldn't stop to pick up the kids. Aimee had any number of excuses, each valid, for her lateness. But Susan wouldn't have it. "If it means your leaving the beach an hour early so that I don't have to wait for you after a full day at work, that's what it's going to have to take," she said. "And if you're late again, I'll wait ten minutes and then I'm leaving. You'll have to walk home from the bus stop." This was no easy feat, since the bus stop is four miles away from our home, and the last two miles are up and down some pretty steep hills.

A week or so passed before Aimee got the urge to go to the beach again. As Susan was dropping her off in the morning at the usual spot, Aimee turned to her and said, "I'll be on time today, even if I have to leave the beach at 4. I sure don't want to walk home."

The funny thing was, Susan had completely forgotten that she had promised such a consequence. But Aimee hadn't.

After so many years of consistent limit setting and follow-through, Aimee knew very well that Susan meant what she said. And she wasn't going to take any chances now.

So you see, even if disciplining your preschooler seems like hard work now, rest assured that your efforts do pay off in the future. Hang in there.

■ ■ ■

Feeling Good About Discipline
CONSEQUENCES PROGRAM

1. Stick to your commitment.
2. Promise to follow through—don't threaten.
3. Intermittent reinforcement is worse than no reinforcment at all.
4. To create consistency in follow-through:
   - Start with small increments.
   - Work as a team.
   - Use lots of praise.
   - Set up the consequence as a choice.
   - Use consequence routinely if an infraction occurs.
   - Give yourself enough time.

CHAPTER SEVEN

Using Positive Reinforcement to Change Behavior

Focusing on the Good, Not the Bad and the Ugly

WHEN YOU THINK ABOUT the process of disciplining your preschooler, you realize that you are really focusing on changing his behavior from unacceptable to acceptable. Indeed, throughout this book, we have been exploring ways to alter your children's negative behavior. Yet it's possible that if you focus on *only* what your kids do wrong, you will miss an important element in the parenting equation—praising them when they get it right!

- "I hate when you do that!"
- "You're bad."
- "You'll never be good enough!"

These are messages that we all give our children when we don't take the time to look for the good in what they do.

Such negative communications will only make your preschooler act out more. He craves your approval, and he will do anything to get your attention, even if it's for behaving in a way that he knows you won't tolerate. This is counterproductive.

In order for you to enjoy the time you spend with your preschooler, you need to make the experience rewarding for all of you. You must find a balance between your role as a disciplinarian and that of a loving parent. You may even need to change some of your habits and ways of approaching problems. If you have grown up in a home where your parents were highly critical, you may have unconsciously adopted their style of relating to your own children. You may need to learn how to emphasize the positive.

By using the guidelines that we suggest for family meetings in Chapter 4 and many of the techniques that follow, you will enhance your child's self-esteem. And you will make your family time together more enjoyable for all of you.

POSITIVE REINFORCEMENT IS A DISCIPLINARY POLICY

When you are persistent in using the recommended discipline program of limit setting, consistent consequence, and follow-through, you will be successful in containing your child's negative behavior. Your preschooler will feel safe and secure in the knowledge that you will not allow him to hurt himself or others.

But is that enough? Are you satisfied to simply halt and contain disruptive and difficult behavior, or would you feel better as a parent if you were able to substitute more acceptable behavior in its place? We think the answer to that question is obvious. Yet substituting new behavior requires work for everyone. It involves teaching on your part and learning on your child's part.

One of the best ways to teach behavior change is to use praise or positive reinforcement. Mitch knows this not only from reading the extensive research on the subject and from studying the clinical evidence in his psychology practice, but also from eight years at the Montebello Intermediate School in East Los Angeles, where he had counseled disadvantaged students. Through his concerted efforts and the intense involvement and commitment of the other administrators, counselors, and teachers, the school was able to establish a program of limits, consistent consequence, and follow-through that was successful in

- reducing truancy by two-thirds.
- eliminating gang violence on or near the campus.
- doing away with all graffiti.
- sending 150 deserving students a years to Disneyland as a reward for their academic achievement, good citizenship, and general attitude improvement.

Indeed, a few years after Mitch left the school district to pursue his private practice, this middle school of 1,500 students, nestled in one of the harshest neighborhoods in Los Angeles, was recognized among the top 25 educational institutions in the country. It received the U.S. Department of Education's National Schools of Excellence Award in 1984. How was it possible to change the behavior and ultimately the lives of so many children?

THE MONTEBELLO EXPERIMENT

Each member of the staff at Montebello Intermediate School played his or her own part in the school's achievement. Since Mitch was in charge of attendance at that time, his role dealt with truancy.

Phase One. Students at most schools are required to have

emergency cards on file with their home phone numbers and their parents' work numbers. Mitch was able to demonstrate to the supervisory personnel that the school would benefit by hiring an additional clerk to call a parent when a child was absent.

Phase Two. Mitch created the limit. He informed the students that truancy was unacceptable. The consequence for an absence was that a parent would be called at home or at work. The new attendance clerk followed through and called a parent on the day of the absence. If the parent was aware that the child was home ill, there was no problem. If, on the other hand, the absence was a truancy, the school set up an appointment for the parents to come in to begin the process of counseling.

This approach is classic limit setting and follow-through, and very shortly it succeeded in reducing truancy at the Montebello Intermediate School. Truants stayed out of school no more than one day at a time (previously, truancies could last from five days to two weeks), and even then they discovered that there wasn't much advantage to their having tricked their parents and school administrators. Once caught, truants would have to deal with the consequence sooner rather than later. Ditching school lost its charm.

The consequence, however, wasn't necessarily punitive. Many times children skip school because of familial, academic, and emotional problems. When the class-cutters returned to school the next day, they had the opportunity to meet with a counselor to discuss their difficulties with their parents and teachers. The counselors would listen to the kids and try to help them to get their needs met. In fact, Mitch established two to three counseling groups a week at the school designed expressly to help these problem students. The students felt valued because their struggles were taken seriously. Giving kids attention in a positive manner increased attendance.

Phase Three. At the same time, other administrators at the school had instituted an incentive program. This was a form of positive reinforcement by which the students earned points for things that they did well, such as:

- reading books.
- displaying good citizenship.
- participating in school activities (sports, the student council, and so on).
- picking up paper.
- reporting unsafe conditions.
- academic achievement.
- improved attendance.

It was possible for any student to generate points for himself at any time. The points would lead to a number of rewards, ranging from ice cream, pizza parties, and movies to a trip to Disneyland.

To appreciate the effectiveness of this one-two punch system for behavior change, we can follow the story of one student. Juan was often late or truant. At the age of thirteen, he was already involved in gangs. Despite his protests to the contrary, it was clear that Juan was always present when anything bad happened, and the other students looked up to him. In fact, he was the type of kid who would throw a quarter into a crowd, then stand back and laugh while everyone dove and stomped for it. But Juan was a "reluctant" leader— that is, if anything bad happened, he was always the first to say, "Not me, man, it was the other guy! I didn't do nothin'."

Mitch worked out a system for Juan. If he was late, absent, or around when a problem occurred, he was considered part of the problem, no matter what he said. After each incident, there would be one of several possible consequences: a call to his parents, an assignment to wash graffiti from the bathroom walls or pick up paper, or a face-to-face confrontation with his parents in a conference. If, however, a problem was impending and he informed a teacher or administrator, he received incentive points and a commendation letter to take home to his parents.

As you can expect, the first three to four weeks were rough going. Juan tested the limits at every turn, to the point where he was even suspended. But then he began to improve. He left little notes for the counseling staff, informing them that a fight or other problem was about to occur.

When Juan started responding to positive reinforcement as a result of the limit setting, consistent consequence, and follow-through, he began to open up to Mitch about his problems. He revealed that his father was an alcoholic, who would awaken the family in the middle of the night when he returned from a drinking binge. Juan was often late for school because he hadn't gotten enough sleep the night before or because he was so upset about his family situation that he just couldn't go out and face the world. In addition, his mother left the house early and came home late at night; she was working as a housekeeper in order to pay the bills. Juan was responsible for getting his younger sisters and brothers ready for school.

As the school staff got to know Juan and his family better they were able to help him. Mitch held conferences with Juan and his father and mother and set up a program of family counseling outside the school setting. When Juan was late, his teachers allowed him to make up work after school.

From the intensive meetings it became clear that Juan suffered educational problems as well. He was good in math, but his reading skills were uneven because of his spotty attendance. The administrators were able to diagnose and treat his educational deficits once they became aware of the problem.

Indeed, as Juan became more successful at school, he involved himself more fully and positively in school activities. He joined the basketball team and the dance committee and was eventually elected to the student council. As an eighth grader, he graduated as the most improved student of his class.

Using the program of setting limits, consistent consequence, and follow-through, coupled with positive reinforcement, Mitch and the other administrators at Montebello Intermediate School were able to halt Juan's negative and destructive behavior and help guide him toward being a model for the rest of the school.

GETTING BACK TO YOUR PRESCHOOLER

How does Mitch's experience as a school administrator translate into child-rearing practices for your preschooler? While you're not running a school, we are sure that you are concerned about making positive changes in your preschooler's behavior. Instituting a discipline program of limit setting, consistent consequence, and follow-through, along with positive reinforcement, will help you make these changes.

Here are the steps that you need to follow in order to be successful:

1. *Assess which behavior you want to change.* It could be a minor problem, from leaving the cap off the tube of toothpaste to a more serious issue such as breaking free of your hand in a busy parking lot or fighting with a sibling. Your job here is to focus on one behavior at a time. To do more may prove to be too confusing for your child and too difficult for you to keep reins on. Decide which behavior you want to change first and work on that until you feel successful.

2. *Eliminate the negative behavior.* Use limits, consistent consequence, and follow-through to stop a behavior that you find unacceptable. Hold family meetings, stick to your consequence, and be fair yet firm. Remember, you're doing this for your child's good.

3. *Use constructive criticism as a way to begin change.* Once

you've gotten the negative behavior under control, you can begin to work toward positive behavior by using *constructive criticism*. Constructive criticism praises your child's accomplishments while it suggests one desirable improvement that you child can easily adapt.

Suppose your four-year-old, Allison, has attempted to clean up her toys from the living room and has slowed down or quit along the way. She has only completed half the task. You could say, "Why are you stopping now? How many times do I have to tell you to put your stuff away? Look, you left all of your blocks over there by the couch. And your markers are still spread all over the table. What are you trying to get away with, anyway?" That kind of criticism may or may not get the job done. Don't bet on it being effective as an encouragement for change. Besides, it's sure to hurt your relationship with your daughter.

On the other hand, using constructive criticism, you could say, "Wow! I see that you are halfway through already. That part of the room looks very nice. You might try bringing the box for your blocks in here so you don't have to make so many trips back and forth to your room. Should I find it for you?" Allison will feel honestly successful regarding the part of the room that she cleaned. Furthermore, she is ready for the next step: guidance and improvement.

When using constructive criticism, make sure to suggest only one improvement at a time. Otherwise, your child may feel overwhelmed by your perception of her shortcomings. Too much constructive criticism begins to sound like plain old criticism.

4. *Learn to accept successive approximations.* When you use positive reinforcement and constructive criticism systematically and repeatedly, you can change your child's behavior slowly over time. This is called the process of *successive approximations*. That means that each time your child attempts

a task the way you want it done, you should give him praise—
whether or not he has completed the task successfully. Give positive reinforcement (praise) to anything that resembles the
desirable behavior at first. Then gradually increase your standards. Eventually, your child will learn to behave in a way
that's close to what you had originally intended.

Make sure, however, that you don't rush the process. There
is a danger that you may expect to move too quickly to the
desired goal. If you become irritable or push your child for-
ward with criticism, you may undermine the ground that
you've gained. Patience is the key here.

Let's go back to our example of Allison cleaning up her
toys from the living room. Remember, she has cleared away
one side but has still left blocks and markers lying around.
You decide to focus on her accomplishments.

"Wow, Allison. You did a wonderful job picking up your
stuffed animals and dollhouse." Paying no attention to the
markers, you conclude, "When you get those blocks put away,
the living room will look great."

You've made an honest statement, and you can feel satisfied that it's sufficient for the moment for Allison to finish
part of the task. She may, in fact, notice that the markers are
still out and start to put them away without your prompting.
If she doesn't, however, she still has gotten closer to your request than before. With the blocks gone, the living room is
better than it was previously, even if it's not perfect. Perhaps
next time she will do more. In fact, before she even begins
the cleanup the following day, you can remind her of the
virtues of bringing the blocks box along. Eventually, she'll
accomplish the whole task on her own.

The use of successive approximations is most appropriate
when you child is not endangering himself or others. If you
want to keep him from playing in the street, you will have to
take stronger measures than merely praising him each time

he gets close to the curb! You may have to restrict him from playing outside for a given period of time until he can handle dealing with the street. Use your good judgment.

5. *Use praise lavishly.* Praise is a powerful self-esteem builder and teaching tool. Praise your child when he accomplishes something important to *himself*, as well as when he has completed a task important to *you.* Your attention to his achievements and accomplishments will validate the significance of what he has done. On the other hand, if you ignore his accomplishments, you will diminish their importance in his eyes. The daily validation of your child's achievements is important to building his self-esteem and changing his negative behavior to something more acceptable.

Say things like

- "I love how you tied your shoes today."
- "You did a wonderful job getting ready this morning."
- "See, we've gotten here on time!"
- "You did a great job cleaning up your room today without my even having to ask!"
- "You and Melissa got along so well today. That's fantastic!"
- "Wow! You finished your dinner with the rest of us!"
- "What a big girl you're getting to be."

In her book *How to Have a Smarter Baby*, Dr. Susan Ludington-Hoe talks at length about using praise and positive reinforcement with infants. What she says about babies can also be applied to your preschooler:

There are those who believe that praise makes people lazy. I am not among them! From my experience and from research, it is clear that a word of encouragement produces more positive behavior. You can remember that from your school days. One A would motivate you to try for more. And at work, a pat on the back from the boss is almost as valuable as a raise to get you to work harder. . . . Be liberal with your praise to your [child]. You will want to praise (and therefore reinforce) [your child's] attempts as well as his successes and any activity that you would like him to continue.

She suggests three potent reinforcers of behavior:

A Look: Eye-to-eye and face-to-face.
A Word: Warm praise . . .
A Touch: You only touch people you really care about. Touch is a very strong communicator of feelings.

When you're putting your son to bed tonight, sit next to him, place your hand on his shoulder or head, and tell him what a great job he did (at something that he attempted). You'll both feel wonderful about it.

THINGS YOU SHOULDN'T SAY
TO YOUR PRESCHOOLER

It's important for you to learn how to praise your child in order to encourage him to make positive changes in his behavior. It's equally important for you to recognize when words that you use thoughtlessly and in anger can be detrimental to that process.

There are many expressions that parents allow to escape their lips without really meaning them and without taking the time to think about the impact that their statements have on their children. Remember, your kids are sensitive. Their emotions are as keenly developed as yours, even if children are not as skilled in expressing their feelings as you may be. Perhaps you can remember thoughtless words or deeds that hurt you at the tender young age of three, four, or five.

Here are some expressions that are particularly painful. Proceed with caution and with love:

1. *"Do what I say because I say so."* You know you hated this coming from your parents. Don't perpetuate it on your child! "Because I say so" emphasizes the power of the person in authority. It is an autocratic way to relate to your child, which will not bring the desired result because no mutual respect is implied. Instead, it can engender her rebellion, the desire for revenge, sneakiness, and irresponsibility. By attempting to crush her will, you may prompt your preschooler to try to get around you in any way possible. At the other extreme, if your child becomes ultraobedient and does what you say because you say so, she may never learn to take the initiative or the responsibility for her own actions.

2. *"I'll show you. You deserve what you're getting."* What could this possibly mean: No child deserves bad things to befall him. And what could you possibly show? That you're stronger? Bigger? We already know that. These expressions lead to resentment, the wish for revenge, rebellion, and fear.

3. *"You're bad."* In Chapter 4, we discussed calling your child bad as an inappropriate approach. Naughty fits right in with that scheme. Both expressions label your child. They imply a moral judgment. When you use these words, your preschooler may feel hopeless about ever improving your view of him. He may feel duty-bound to live up to your negative expectations. He will experience hurt and shame.

4. *"You'll never learn"* or *"I'll never forget."* Using *always* and *never* made your child feel as if his misdeeds are cast in bronze. These particular expressions emphasize past negative behavior. They make your child feel unacceptable and rob him of the hope of ever redeeming himself. He learns to live with the fact that he has permanent undesirable traits.

5. *"No child of mine would do a thing like that!"* Could your four-year-old's misdeed be so bad that you disown her? Come on! You are conveying the hidden message that your child

is unacceptable unless she is your clone. This, as we all know, is impossible. She is an individual, separate from you. Again, this expression will make her feel rebellious, frightened, and vengeful.

6. *"My convenience is more important than your feelings."* No one likes to feel discounted, not even your three-year-old. He will become rebellious and defiant if you shun him aside often enough. Worse yet, he will find ways to sabotage your actions. He will show you that his feelings certainly do have importance, whether or not you care to pay attention to them. In fact, he'll find all kinds of ways to make his anger known to you.

THINGS YOU *SHOULD* SAY TO YOUR PRESCHOOLER

Just as there are expressions you should avoid, so there are ways of approaching your children that you would do well to adopt. These statements communicate your love, trust, and respect, as you both work toward change. In return, they engender your child's love, trust, and respect for you. Parenting is often a two-way street. In biblical terms, you reap what you sow.

1. *"I trust you to learn to respect the rights of others."* Instead of being authoritarian and usurping your child's rights, this statement encourages his cooperation and respect for himself and the rights of others. It also enhances his feelings of self-discipline. He may be thinking, "If Dad trusts that I can do this, then maybe I really can." You are presenting a positive model of how the world works.

2. *"You are capable of deciding"* or *"I trust you to make good choices."* Either of these statements is great to use when you are presenting limits and consequences. If your child chooses the consequence because he can't control himself (no dessert for two days because he sneaked cookies), he learns from his

experience that the choice he made is logically related to his misbehavior. Since he had a hand in the outcome, he participates willingly rather than under duress and coercion. Your faith that he can make good choices helps to increase his feelings of resourcefulness.

3. *"You are a worthwhile person. What happens to you really matters to me."* Your child will sense from this that she is acceptable and lovable even though her act (poking her sister) is not. You communicate your caring and concern.

4. *"I don't like what you are doing, but I still love you."* This is another statement that helps to separate the deed from the person. When you communicate this information to your child with respect and goodwill in your voice and heart, he will feel secure about your love and support, even though he knows he was wrong in misbehaving.

It's easy and makes good sense to combine all of these statements when you are discussing a consequence with your child. You can say, for example, "Linda, you are a worthwhile person. What happens to you matters to me. I would like to see you be able to get along well with others. That's why it's not OK for you to poke Beth. If you poke her again, you will choose to have me move you into another room. I know you can make the responsible choice. I trust you to learn to respect the rights of others."

In the long run, effective discipline and positive reinforcement enhance each other. They work together in a synergistic system to change your child's negative behavior into something that you can all live with, promoting security, satisfaction, and achievement.

■ ■ ■

Feeling Good About Discipline
THE POSITIVE-REINFORCEMENT PROGRAM

1. Negative communications make your child act out more.
2. Discipline means changing behavior.
3. Use positive reinforcement as a tool to make that change:
   - Assess what behavior you want to change.
   - Eliminate negative behavior using limits, consequences, and follow-through.
   - Use constructive criticism to begin moving toward positive behavior.
   - Accept successive approximations.
4. Expressions you shouldn't use with your preschooler:
   - "Do what I say because I say so."
   - "I'll show you. You deserve what you're getting."
   - "You're bad."
   - "You'll never learn" or "I'll never forget."
   - "No child of mine would do a thing like that."
   - "My convenience is more important than your feelings."
5. Expressions you should use with your preschooler:
   - "I trust you to learn to respect the rights of others."
   - "You are capable of deciding" or "I trust you to make good choices."
   - "You are a worthwhile person. What happens to you really matters to me."
   - "I don't like what you're doing, but I still love you."

CHAPTER EIGHT

Laughter is the Best Medicine

W<small>HEN</small> C<small>HERIE AND</small> A<small>IMEE</small> were seven and four years old respectively, we had come to the end of our collective parental rope. Certainly we loved our daughters as much as any parents possibly could. We wanted them to care about one another with the same intensity that we loved each of them. We longed for ours to be a happy household in which our kids listened to us and everyone got along in relative harmony a la Ozzie and Harriet. What a pipe dream!

In truth, Cherie did not take kindly to the intrusion of her baby sister into our family (see Chapter 12). And as our kids grew older, she made a habit of cutting Aimee off in midsentence, belittling her and swatting her away, as if she were an insignificant and annoying fly. As a preschooler, Aimee so wanted to play with and be loved by her older sister that she ignored the attacks and kept coming back for more, much like those weighted, round-bottomed dolls that instantly bounce back after you've knocked them over.

Mealtimes—an occasion when we all came together as a family—seemed to be the worst. Each child vied for our attention at the expense of the other. They interrupted one another, they whined, they yelled, they teased. And no amount of our pleading and cajoling for order seemed to make a difference. Dinner was enough to send us both in search of Maalox.

Yet, as irritating as Cherie and Aimee's bickering was to us, we recognized that underlying it, both children were in pain. Cherie felt displaced, while Aimee felt put down. How could we let them know that we understood their feelings but still couldn't tolerate their behavior?

One Sunday morning, Mitch had an idea. The best defense is a good offense. After setting the table and frying up a batch of our usual weekend French toast, we called the girls in for breakfast. Tearing themselves away from their morning cartoons, they were struck dumb when they entered the kitchen and found us sitting in "their" seats.

"I was here first," Susan whined at Mitch.

"No, that's my seat," Mitch snapped back. "Give it back!" He turned to Cherie, "Mommy, make her give it back! She's always taking my things."

For a moment, the kids seemed bewildered. Had we gone mad? But then they understood the game. Cherie climbed into Susan's seat, ready to take on her personality while Aimee got to play Daddy. In the meantime, we parents had a ball. We interrupted one another. We complained and criticized. We blamed and tattled. Our kids giggled at our shenanigans while they also squirmed in recognition. The play-acting hit home.

Cherie tried to maintain order using Susan's approach— pleading. When that didn't work, Aimee yelled in an appropriately paternal voice. It hardly helped. Not only had we finally gotten their attention, but we had also gotten through to them. They had vicariously experienced the feelings of irritation and helplessness that their fighting had engendered in us.

After this moment of recognition, we were all able to have a great conversation about their relationship and family communication over our cold French toast and maple syrup. Success at last.

THE VALUE OF HUMOR

Effective discipline occurs when you are able to communicate with your children on their level. Laughter, play, and a light touch are gentle but effective ways to open communication. They put you and your youngsters at ease while they help you enter your children's inner world.

During play, your preschoolers are guilelessly involved in the nonverbal expression of their feelings. If you pay close attention (we'll show you what to look for), you may be able to discern how Dana perceives you and other family members as well as the important developmental issues she may be struggling to overcome. In addition, play is a marvelous way for a child to release pent-up emotions such as anger and resentment in a constructive way. Humor, moreover, can enhance your warm, close relationship with your kids while you deliver some feedback that they'd be resistant to hearing under more strained circumstances. Indeed, as long as you're laughing at the situation and not the person, humorous interactions help to de-escalate conflicts, reduce family stress, and place problems in perspective. It's hard to stay mad at each other if you're all holding your sides from giggling. Besides, as we've learned from research psychologists at Loma Linda University in California (who validated Dr. Norman Cousins' theories as stated in his book, *Anatomy of An Illness*), laughter creates chemical changes in the brain that release endorphins, the body's own pain-killers. It is, indeed, the best medicine.

HOW TO USE PLAY TO
DISCIPLINE YOUR PRESCHOOLER

Many psychologists who work with children use what they call "play therapy" to understand their young patients' issues. Using puppets, clay, papers and crayons as well as small sandboxes filled with toy characters of all sorts, and storytelling, they engage the children in imaginative games to ascertain what's on their minds.

While most parents aren't formally trained psychologists, they can learn ways to understand their children's world from these techniques. Just bear two principles in mind:

1. *You don't have to interpret your child's behavior.* The simple act of playing together helps you to communicate with your preschooler because you are bonding and connecting with one another. He, in turn, will let you into his inner world during the game, thereby giving you hints about what is important to him and what he's struggling to overcome.

2. *Avoid judgmental and critical statements.* During play, your child may express feelings that might not normally emerge in conversation with you. At those times, he is aware enough of your needs and biases to understand what you find unacceptable and so he may avoid certain topics. During a game, however, he may let down his defenses and express his real emotions, some of which might disturb you. In that case, you would be wise to avoid criticizing his feelings. Remember, all feelings and fantasies are accepted. It's the behavior in the real world that might need changing.

If during play, your son makes the baby doggy bit off the head of the daddy doggy, rather than jumping in with, "Oh, that's terrible! How could you do such a bad thing!" you can say, "Wow! It looks to me as if the baby doggy is really angry at the daddy doggy. Why do you think he's so angry?" If you criticize your child's fantasy and feelings, he may withdraw from you. Rather, use the playtime to discover what's upsetting to him.

It's perfectly acceptable for preschoolers to play out their issues in fantasy. Let's look at some games that encourage your children's expression of emotion.

PUPPETS

Puppets can help you and your kids express feelings that have gone unspoken and issues that have resisted resolution. They are great for storytelling, especially with preschoolers. If you're the puppeteer, you can imbue your puppet with all sorts of characteristics that you'd like to teach your child such as neatness, cooperation, honesty, and openness. Puppets can help you get your point of view across to your child without your sounding overly parental and authoritarian and thus, engendering his resentment.

Aimee's favorite puppet was a ratty gray mouse with a red and white polka dot bow tie that she ingeniously dubbed "Puppet Mousie." We could show Mousie how to brush his teeth or put away his toys. He was always cooperative with us. And when he told Aimee how she should brush her teeth and put away her toys in his special high squeaky voice, she was apt to follow his directions. He was in the habit of giving her a kiss if she cooperated.

Your youngsters can use puppets for their own needs, as well. These toys can help them to express feelings they might otherwise have difficulty putting into words. When Aimee was born, for example, we bought Cherie, then three-and-a-half, a Cookie Monster puppet—only we called him the "Attention Monster." Whenever Cherie felt left out, she would run for her "Attention Monster" who would growl at Susan in his primordial way, "Me want attention! Me want attention!" Sometimes, Susan could accommodate Cherie's vicarious demand. When she couldn't, she thanked her blue, furry friend for letting her know how he felt, then informed him that she would give both he and Cherie attention just as soon as she could.

Kids love to play with puppets because they can easily control them. Even if your youngster's hands are too small to manipulate the puppet's arms, her fingers can still work the head and mouth. Finger puppets are ideal for young children. Indeed, you can create a whole family of finger puppets to act out small domestic situation comedies based on themes in your own family. Kids feel free to give advice to puppets (in fact, you can stop the action and ask your child, "What do you think Lion should do?"), and they even enjoy arguing with them.

CLAY

Clay is a marvelous medium for self-expression because it is infinitely malleable. With your youngsters, you can create families of snails or worms who interact with one another in much the same way as your family does. As with puppets, clay play can help you to discover what's on your preschooler's mind. Indeed, your kids can also express their anger at siblings (or you) by squashing the clay representations of them. Remember to refrain from critical comments, should this occur. Simply regard your child's activity as a way for you to gain information.

During the course of play therapy in his office, for example, Mitch watched his young patient symbolically express anger while using clay and puppets. Jeffrey had designed a clay birthday cake dinner for two puppets—one he designated the old brother and the other, the baby sister. With a surprising lack of guile, Jeffrey unceremoniously dumped the baby sister puppet in the trash, while the big brother puppet proceeded to stuff all of the clay birthday cake into his own mouth. From this interaction, it was clear to Mitch that Jeffrey wanted to feel special within his family and he certainly needed more attention from his parents.

Once your child reveals such information, you can gently guide him into a conversation about his feelings by restating his emotions and using mirroring (see Chapter 4). Of course, if all else fails, kids can also release loads of pent-up anger by squeezing and pounding clay into paper-thin pancakes. If nothing else, it feels great!

CRAYONS

You'll find play with crayons and paper helps your child to express his emotions, as well. Children project themselves—their feelings, aspirations, fantasies—into their artwork and so reveal themselves indirectly. One of Mitch's favorite games with our girls was what he called the "Squiggle game." He and our daughters would all create an abstract design scribbling all over a sheet of paper. Then, each would pick out a shape and talk about what it reminded them of, much as kids like to ascribe shapes of animals and toys to clouds.

Sometimes, if youngsters persist in finding a series of negative images (guns, fire, explosions, smoke, smashed cars, and dead bodies) it might be wise to question where these perceptions come from. Perhaps television news reports of war and mayhem have made a deeper impression on your child than you thought. In such instances, it's advisable to have your preschooler talk about his fears and his feelings while you reassure him of his safety. You might even encourage him to use crayons to express his feelings more directly. Recurrent nightmares and fears—especially if they revolve around a family tragedy or natural disaster—may warrant several visits with a qualified child therapist.

You might also want to watch out for other revealing details in your youngster's art. If a child draws a picture of family members in disproportionate sizes (daddy looks like a giant next to mommy and the kids), he may be expressing his perception of who is in power (or by whom he feels threatened) in the family. The predominance of the colors red and black can be evocative of the feelings of anger and sorrow. Hard, angry scribbling is great for releasing rage while rigid and repetitive drawing may indicate a child's need for control in a chaotic environment. Before making any interpretation about the meaning of your child's artwork, ask him what he is drawing or showing.

Even the way a child uses a coloring book may hint at his state of mind. While the ability to color inside the lines is a matter of eye-hand coordination and developmental maturity, how a child perceives of and expresses his "mistakes" can inform you of his expectations for himself, his level of self-criticism, or any early tendency toward perfectionism. By the way, should your child be overly critical of his own artwork, it's more helpful for you to ask, "Oh, why do you think your painting is terrible? . . . I see. How would you do it differently next time?" than to reassure him with statements that ultimately deny his feelings such as, "You shouldn't say that. It's a wonderful painting."

DOLLS AND PLAY FIGURES

Much like puppets and clay, you and your child can set dolls up into families and watch how family conflicts play themselves out. Kids' play with dolls reflects the world as they perceive it. We remember one incident during the free-wheeling 1970s when many of our friends were living together without benefit of marriage licenses, in which five-year-old Cherie complained about the set-up in her new Barbie New York penthouse apartment. "Where's Ken going to sleep when he stays over?" she asked, pointing to the single bed that came with the dollhouse.

In her play, Cherie was acting out a situation that she had encountered. How did we respond? Well, although we were a little shocked by her perceptiveness, we didn't want to make an issue of it. Instead, we simply said: "That's an interesting question, Cherie. Where do you think Ken should sleep?" She made a place for him on the living room sofa.

STORYTELLING

Many of Lillian Hoban's books such as *Bread and Jam for Francis* and *Bedtime for Francis* address issues that you're bound to encounter with your preschooler—balkiness at mealtime and bedtime. In these timeless tales, animals act out perennial family issues of limit setting, testing, and natural consequences. We found them most helpful in conveying to our daughters appropriate guidelines for behavior. But storytelling need not be limited to reading certain books. You can make up your own stories, based on your experiences growing up, as a way of sharing your life with your children and teaching them.

Preschoolers respond to animal characters, and so you can set your story in a forest or jungle—or even in the city—much as Lillian Hoban does. The fables that your create can convey valuable lessons about values, responsibility, and honesty.

Likewise, encourage your kids to make up their own stories. In addition to enhancing their creativity, their tales will also let you into parts of their lives that they feel are important. You can have them dictate their tales to you. After they illustrate their stories, the stapled pages make a great "book" that you'll enjoy reading ten years hence.

Taken together, these five techniques will open windows into your children's inner reality. And, of course, sometimes a good game of tag or touch football or a tumbling, giggle-induced session of roughhousing can release tension and create great rapport even when feelings have been hurt.

THE DEVELOPMENTAL STAGES OF HUMOR

Dr. Lawrence Kutner explains in his excellent book, *Parent & Child: Getting Through to Each Other*, that "The things that children find funny tell us a great deal about their level of development and what is on their minds. . . . [This] explains why three-year-olds, who are often still mastering toilet training, are enthralled by 'bathroom' humor while seven-year-olds, who no longer consider toilet training an issue, think such jokes are just stupid." And it also explains why an eighteen-month-old, when presented with a joke about bodily functions, wouldn't have a clue!

When we understand what our children find funny, we can use humor to better reach them. One-year-olds, for instance, are usually enthralled by games of peek-a-boo. At this age, your child is still mastering the concept of object constancy—that is, that an object (such as a parent) still exists, even if he can't see it. This is an important part of his learning about who he is.

Young preschoolers are learning that the world is arranged with a certain orderliness. Visual jokes that play on disorder (for instance, our daughter Cherie used to delight in putting her training pants on her head) will appeal to his sense of humor. And, as we mentioned above, they are also prone to making jokes relating to bodily and bathroom functions. While these quips might embarrass you in mixed company, they are a normal part of your child coming to grips with controlling his body and should not be made a source of shame or disparagement. Kids between four and five love to giggle as they make up funny words and faces, take pratfalls, and begin to tell simple "knock-knock" jokes.

By the age of six, youngsters develop a more sophisticated sense of humor. Since they are learning to deal with abstract concepts and the intricacies of language, their favorite riddles and jokes may revolve around illogical statements and puns such as, "What has four wheels and flies? A garbage truck!"

HOW YOU CAN APPEAL TO
YOUR CHILD'S SENSE OF HUMOR

You can use humor to discipline your preschooler. Even one-year-olds respond to jokes! We remember Cherie at that age shrieking with delight when we pretended to suck on her pacifier or expressed our love toward it. Child development experts and psychologists suggest various laugh-evoking techniques to reach our kids. Here are some that seem the most effective.

1. *Write notes and draw cartoons.* Preschoolers enjoy received little letters from you. They will ask you to read the notes to them, somehow softening the blow of your demand. You need not be limited to verbal messages. A Post-it stuck onto the bathroom mirror showing a tube of toothpaste with a large knurdle of paste gushing forth may remind your kids to screw on the cap for at least a week or so.

You can even create a cartoon campaign identifying family members as stick figures at various tasks that you'd like your kids to do or refrain from doing. In her book on using humor in the business world, *What Mona Lisa Knew*, Dr. Barbara Mackoff, a management psychologist explains how a business firm could motivate its workers to use safety precautions by featuring cartoon characters who don't abide by safety regulations. You can use similar techniques with your kids for issues that you find important.

Dr. Mackoff even describes how one supervisor entered a meeting of indignant employees with a bull's-eye fastened to his chest as a way to open the discussion of grievances. What a funny lead-in that would make to a family meeting!

2. *Use fantasy.* Giving your youngster what he wants in fantasy if you can't fulfill his wishes in reality is a good way to de-escalate conflicts and power struggles. Fantasy plays help to assuage a youngster's frustrated desires. These fantasies can be outright silly. In fact, the funnier and more outlandish the fantasy, the easier the bitter pill of "No, you can't," may go down.

For example, to the child who wants two donuts (when you know that she shouldn't even be eating one), you can say, "Boy, Lisa, sounds like you really love those chocolate-covered donuts. Bet you'd eat a million of them."

She might laugh and reply, "No, I want two million."

"How about three million?"

"No, four million!"

"How about eighty quadzillion?"

"Yeah! Eighty quadzillion sounds just about right!"

The same technique could be used for the sick youngster who wants to play in the snow on a blustery day ("I wish you could build five snowmen who have a giant snowball fight all over the front yard!") or the recalcitrant preschooler who doesn't want to get dressed when it's time to go to daycare ("I wish you could lay in bed all day today and tomorrow and the next day and watch cartoons.")

3. *Imitate your child and use his imagery.* Dr. Mackoff explains that imitation can be the silliest and most efficacious form of humor among family members. "It offers a loved one," she writes, "a zany, rather than angry, opportunity to examine

his or her behavior without becoming defensive." During our role playing with our children, we used imitation to the very best advantage.

But imitation can take other forms, as well. Some experts now believe, for example that imitating your child's whining helps to eliminate it. When your youngster sees how silly you sound, she's bound to crack up herself and a "real" conversation can ensue. Indeed, Dr. Mackoff even suggests a "Whine-In" business meeting where everyone vents his frustration. Such an event can also take place during one of your family meetings. Let yourselves take five minutes to get your ya-yas out.

Perhaps one of the best ways to imitate your children in good spirit is to use their language. You might get your kids' attention by calling them names that they might dub one another such as dorks, nerds, dweebs or other semi-endearing terms.

In *Loving Your Child Is Not Enough*, parent educator Nancy Samalin shares an example of a mom whose culinary efforts are scorned by her young son. Tommy criticized his mother's gourmet meals with statements such as "This looks yucky," which were quickly followed by hostile arguments and angry dinners. One day, the mother decided to use the technique of imitation when she served a meal of turkey and gravy:

TOMMY: What's this gooey stuff:
MOM: It's mucus!
TOMMY: Ha, ha, ha! It sure does look like it.
MOM: I guess to you it does.
TOMMY: I wonder what would happen if they killed turkeys that had colds and they really could have mucus on them.

Tommy laughed at his own joke and even tasted the gravy. This dinner, in contrast to many earlier ones, proceeded congenially.

4. *Use inside jokes.* Every family has inside jokes and funny made-up words. These short-hand forms of communication promote intimacy and warm feelings within your family because they exclude all others from the jest. We're sure that in the family just described, simply whispering the phrase, "Turkey mucus," would convey a whole set of reactions between Tommy and his mother whenever they took a meal at a friend's house or tried a new restaurant. It might even motivate Tommy to taste something exotic.

Sometimes the in-joke can be the brainchild of the children. In our family, for instance, our teenage daughters teased us about how we predictably (and unconsciously) stationed ourselves each and every time a new boyfriend came to call: Mitch at the doorway and Susan hanging back a bit at the base of the stairs. When the doorbell rang for a first date, our daughters were tempted to shout at us: "OK, everyone, man your battle stations."

5. *Create lists.* In *Loving Your Child Is Not Enough,* Nancy Samalin advises that some parents benefit from keeping "bug lists"—compendia of their children's behaviors that they find irritating or conflict-inducing. She explains that the list helps to put major and minor offenses into perspective and may give parents the opportunity to decide which battles are worth fighting.

But children may also benefit from such catalogs. Mackoff suggests, "When I grow up . . ." lists in which youngsters can enumerate (or you can write for them): "When I grow up, I won't make my kids eat all their peas, clean up their rooms, or be quiet in a restaurant." Indeed, one mother encouraged her children to accomplish the required tasks but then keep a "When I grow up . . ." book whose manuscript grew weekly. (That would be an interesting memento to save and show your grandchildren twenty years from now!) Mackoff also writes of a father who had his children keep a "Saturday list" in which they inscribed the issues they wanted to whine about during the week. (Preschoolers might make drawings of the "offenses.") Every Saturday, he sat down with them to go over their enumeration and more often than not, by then they had forgotten about most of their grievances.

When we use humor to get through to our kids, we should also remember to allow our youngsters to get through to us. Poking fun at ourselves relieves tension. No one, especially children, likes to be around a humorless, serious, stuffed shirt. Let your kids see your silly side and your laughter. Let them know that their jokes and bon mots impact you. When you laugh with one another, even the most difficult problem becomes manageable because you have created a feeling of good will, community, and cooperation. When you're together, you can resolve anything.

■ ■ ■

Feeling Good About Discipline
LAUGHTER AND PLAY

1. Laughter is the best medicine.
2. Use play to discipline your preschooler.
3. Don't interpret your child's behavior.
4. Avoid judgmental or critical statements.
5. Puppets, clay, crayons, dolls, and storytelling help you get your point across while you learn what's on your child's mind.
6. Be sure the humor you use is developmentally appropriate.
7. Appeal to your child's sense of humor by using:
   ■ Notes and cartoons.
   ■ Fantasy.
   ■ His or her own imagery.
   ■ Inside jokes.
   ■ lists.

CHAPTER NINE

Presenting a United Front

Recently a magazine article was brought to our attention. In it the writer, Bette-Jean Raphael, mother of a young boy, complained about how she and her husband differed in style and expectations. She wrote:

My mate, a lawyer by profession, is disciplined, self-contained, and inner-directed. I am as disciplined as a freshly adopted mutt, as self-contained as the Oracle at Delphi, as inner-directed as your average preschooler. He has orderly habits and a demeanor that remains relatively unruffled in the face of everyday problems. My habits are so disorderly that they could more properly be called whims, and I tend to behave as if there *are* no everyday problems, only unmitigated disasters. . . .

However, we refused to let the mere fact that we were ill-suited keep us apart. And over the years, we managed to overcome our diversity enough of the time to be happy together. . . .

This precarious equilibrium received a reverberating jolt when our son Jacob was born. Almost immediately, we found that we couldn't separate our attitudinal differences on child-rearing. Problems arose the first night Jacob spent under our roof.

We are sure that most couples will recognize at least a part of their struggle in this woman's entertaining lament. For in truth, we often marry a person whose character traits complement our own. If we are flighty, we seek out someone who is stable. If we are emotional, we look for a stoic. If we are grounded, earthy, and solid, our perfect partner is spiritual, ephemeral, and spontaneous. It's only natural that child-rearing perspectives will differ in homes with such diverse parents.

Even if we and our mates are not polar opposites as Bette-Jane and her husband seemed to be, we can't help but have conflicting opinions about how to go about the business of being a parent. Janice makes eating broccoli a game: She says, "Look, Danny, the broccoli looks just like a tree. Can you eat the tree?" "The broccoli is a choo-choo train coming into the tunnel. Here it comes, Danny, choo-choo, choo-choo, choo-choo." Steven is all business. He says: "Eat the broccoli, Dan, or there's no dessert." End of story.

Where do these differing parenting styles come from? Most often they are the flowering of seeds planted by our own parents. We as adults repeat (sometimes unwittingly) the way that our own mothers and fathers did the job with us. Sometimes we may even catch ourselves in midsentence, horrified that we sound just like good old Mom or Dad. This can happen, even if we vowed that we're going to do things differently from our parents.

Since our spouses grew up in different homes than ours, they can't possibly approach child-rearing in exactly the same way as we do. They have their own parental ghosts to contend with.

At other times, we may simply have different agendas at the moment. Janice feels that she has too little time to spend with Danny because of her heavy work schedule. She turns mealtime into playtime, because that's the only time she has! Steven, on the other hand, is hungry and tired. He just wants to eat and then relax in front of the TV. He's not interested in fun at the table. Games will have to wait until the weekend, when he and Danny can kick a soccer ball around. Given differences such as these, it is inevitable that conflicts will arise over how to feed Danny his broccoli.

WHY YOU SHOULD WORK AT CREATING A UNITED FRONT

Despite the obvious difficulty, it is imperative that couples work out these differences. Why? First of all, because it's good for your relationship and ultimately your marriage. Conflicts arising around parenting issues often diminish closeness and intimacy between spouses. It's natural to feel distant from the one you love when you feel that he or she holds views very different from your own. You become polarized. If one of you has the correct approach, the other has to be wrong.

It's best for you not to make your differences in discipline style a personal battleground. Most couples will be able to resolve their conflicts if they follow the program we suggest below. If, however, you find it impossible to compromise, you may need more help in the form of professional marriage counseling so that you can each work toward the good of your child and your marriage.

Second, it's important to create a feeling of consensus because it's crucial for your children. Kids are excellent detectives. They will sniff out inconsistencies, chinks in the armor, and conflicts. Once they sense a weak spot, they will try to use this for all it's worth to satisfy their own needs. The classic case is that of the child who figures out how to play one parent against the other.

Tracy has very strict rules about eating before meals. Her son Benjy knows those rules because he comes up against them everyday. But on Saturday, Daddy is home, and Benjy knows that Daddy is a real pushover. At 4:30 in the afternoon, Benjy asks his mom for a Popsicle, knowing full well that his request will be denied. Predictably, she tells him, "No. It's too close to dinner. You can have one after we eat. I don't want you to spoil your appetite."

Benjy is not perturbed. He approaches Mark, who is splayed out on the hammock in the backyard. "Daddy, can I have a Popsicle?"

"Sure, son. Go ahead."

Three minutes later, Benjy marches through the house, triumphantly displaying the prize for his mother to see. "Benjy," she cries in dismay, "I thought I told you no sweets now. Put that back in the freezer until later, or you get no dessert for two days."

"But Mommy," Benjy replies, "Daddy said it was OK. I asked him, and he said, 'Go ahead.'"

"He did? What right has he got to tell you that?" Now Tracy is incensed. She seeks out her husband to excoriate him. Doesn't he know that Benjy isn't allowed any sweets before dinner? Doesn't he know that he's undermining all of her hard work in setting up rules in the house? Can't he co-operate with her just once instead of making her life harder?

These, of course, are fighting words. Mark hardens in his position. "What's the big deal? It's hot. I thought the kid could have a treat. It's not a crime, you know. I can't be-lieve what a big deal you're making over a little thing."

"Little? What are you calling little? You know, you're just like your dad. Lackadaisical. You don't care what happens to me or your son."

And there you go. Maybe this is a little extreme, but you get the picture. While Tracy and Mark are arguing, Benjy happily sucks on his Popsicle. He knows his way around his parents. And he knows how to get himself off the hook.

Although Benjy may seem satisfied that he's gotten the bests of his parents, this kind of manipulation may hurt him in the long run. It can be damaging for Mark and Tracy to argue about Benjy's discipline in front of the little boy. He may be confused by their anger and differing points of view. He may feel forced to choose sides. After having lit the fuse, he may feel frightened by the force of the explosion that his mischievous act prompted.

When Cherie and Aimee were preschoolers—and even today for that matter—we tried as hard as we could to settle such arguments out of the children's earshot. Sometimes this meant that one of us had to force himself or herself to stay silent while the other was doling out a disciplinary measure with which the spouse disagreed. Not interrupting in this case is not easy and requires discipline. Yet we felt that we shouldn't argue about the discipline in front of the disciplinee. We resolved our differences later!

In Benjy's case, it was best for all concerned to present a united front to the little boy. Tracy should have taken Mark aside to discuss her feelings about treats before dinner. One would hope that the two of them would come up with something like, "*Mom and I talked it over, and we agree that from now on . . .*" That kind of statement makes it very clear that both parents are on the same side of the issue. The child has very little room to squirm away from what is expected of him. And he also feels safer in that he senses his parents are in accord.

HOW DO YOU RESOLVE THE DIFFERENCES?

Conflicts over parenting styles can affect all aspects of your relationship with your spouse. Here are some tips to help you resolve them:

1. *Approach the issue with a spirit of cooperation and equality.* Rather than your taking the position that you're right (and your spouse absolutely wrong), rather than you arguing your case as if to convince 240 million Americans and your spouse of the rectitude of your beliefs, you will need to open the discussion with the attitude that you each have valuable ideas. You each have something important to add to the discussion. You're just coming to the problem from different perspectives.

2. *Make a list.* In his practice, Mitch uses a straightforward approach to open the lines of communication between spouses when conflicting parenting styles tear at the fabric of their family. This helps to make apparent and conscious needs that had been hidden or previously only understood.

At one of their family-therapy sessions Mitch asks each parent to write out a formal list of his or her disciplining goals. Tracy and Mark are prime candidates for such an exercise. Here's what Mark's list looked like:

Mark's List

- "I want Benjy to love me."
- "I want him to express himself freely."
- "I want to feel close to him."
- "I want him to grow up to be an individual."
- "I don't want to cramp his style."
- "I want him to have fun."
- "I don't want him to have a relationship with me like the one I had with my dad—that was no relationship at all!"
- "I want my son to be disciplined. I want him to act appropriately."
- "I want Benjy to listen to me because he loves me."

From this list, it is easy to see why Mark was happy to grant Benjy his request for a Popsicle. It was an act of love and playfulness.

Now let's look at Tracy's goals:

Tracy's List
- "I want to be close to my son."
- "Running the house efficiently is important to me."
- "Benjy's acting out makes my job difficult. It want him to stop acting out."
- "I like to feel in charge."
- "I want to protect my child from danger and make sure that he grows up to be a healthy, strong adult."
- "I want my son to love me and to listen to me because I'm his mother."
- "I don't want to feel undermined when I set up rules in the house. I want Benjy to follow rules for his own safety and my peace of mind."

3. *Compare and analyze your list.* The mere act of writing down your goals helps a great deal, because you bring out into the open your hidden agendas and needs, which are often different from your spouse's. This begins the process of communication so important to creating a united front. In comparing your lists, look to see where you have areas of agreement and where your ideas clash.

When you compare Mark's list with Tracy's, it's easy to see why they fall into conflicts about how to parent Benjy. Tracy sees discipline as a way to create order in her house. She believes in a fixed set of rules to help chart the way. She likes to be in command and in control. This is her means of coming to grips with a world that she perceives as essentially random, dangerous, and unpredictable. In one small corner of her universe—her home—there will be semblance of structure. Tracy is going to do everything in her power to see that this is achieved.

Mark, on the other hand, has adopted a laissez-faire style of parenting. He wants Benjy to develop as an individual at his own pace rather than fit within a predetermined structure. Therefore, rugged individualism is more important to him than rules are. He wants to negotiate and work things out. He seems to desperately crave the love of his son as a way to make up for the deficits in his relationship with his own father. He may be willing to forgo the rules as a way to gain his son's positive regard.

At first glance, Mark and Tracy seem poles apart. Yet, from comparing and analyzing these lists, it's also clear that both Mark and Tracy love their son and want the best for him. They want him to act appropriately and to listen to them. This common ground is a great place to start a discussion. Mark and Tracy, in essence, want to achieve the same general goals, but they are coming at them from differing points of view.

4. *Cross off the goals you have in common.* Both Mark and Tracy could agree that raising a healthy child was a valuable goal for them to pursue. That was a good goal to have in common. They didn't need to work on it. Once they recognized where their feelings and ideas overlapped, it was easy to set those aside so that they could focus on areas over which they disagreed. Those are the ones that needed to be worked on.

5. *Focus on one area at a time to work out a solution.* Mark and Tracy chose one point that was the least emotionally charged—snacks before dinnertime. They tried to work out a compromise that the whole family could live with.

6. *Keep an open mind.* Now Mark and Tracy reviewed their feelings about the issue of snacks before dinnertime with these thoughts in mind:

- Limit setting and discipline are negotiable between spouses.
- Intimacy increases when you create a meeting of the minds for both points of view.
- Each person has the "right" way.

Where approaches and perspectives diverge, they were able to make a commitment to work out some compromises.

They each asked themselves, "What approaches can I live with that my partner has to offer?" and "What do I find intolerable?"

During their discussion, Mark came to see Tracy's rules about mealtime as an extension of their mutual desire to raise a healthy child. He then was willing to go along with her "no sweets after 4:00 P.M." ruling. He promised to back her up the next time Benjy tried to wheedle some goodies out of him after the appointed time.

And Tracy realized that Mark's giving in was not a sign of weakness, laziness, or lack of caring on his part. It became clear to her that her husband wanted to please their son in any way he could, because he loved him so much. The Popsicle was merely a harmless sign of Mark's affection for his son.

Mark and Tracy were able to sort out their feelings about the snacktime issue and see that they did agree on crucial points. Their differing parenting styles no longer seemed to be an issue. This strengthened their feelings of love toward each other and helped them to keep their manipulative child in check. All in all, their efforts to present a united front created a greater sense of peace and cooperation within their family.

Presenting a united front to your child means that you've been successful in resolving conflicting points of view in advance and out of sight of your children. Remember, these conflicts can affect all aspects of your relationship, from equality and intimacy to family bonding. Take them seriously and work them through.

WHAT IF YOU'RE DIVORCED?

It's difficult to discuss presenting a united front if you are no longer united in matrimony. Divorced couples are as different, one to the next, as are married ones. Each couple has its own way of resolving or not resolving their differences.

Some ex-spouses who share custody of their children are capable of maintaining close ties and cooperate with each other in child-rearing practices. Others continue to war bitterly for decades and use their different parenting styles to curry the favor of the child, who is caught in the middle. And there are all degrees of variation between these two extremes. Divorce can sometimes be a messy business.

From the point of view of security, children prefer one system of discipline. This, however, is not always possible. If divorced or separated spouses are unwilling or unable to communicate with each other amicably, and they decide, instead, to hold to their individual discipline styles, their children may become confused. They get differing messages and values from the two households.

How can you handle this dilemma constructively? Probably the best way to deal with your child's complaints, "But at Mom's house we can . . ." is to validate his feelings with mirroring. You can say, "I know it's confusing to have two sets of rules, but that's just the way it is. It may be hard at first, but after a while you'll get used to it. I know that Mom lets you go to bed at 8 o'clock. But at my house, bedtime is at 7:30. Mom loves you, and so do I. We just have different ways of doing things.

The world is very complex, and we all have to make adjustments. But children are amazingly resilient. Just as they can adjust to the change in rules when they move from one classroom to another, so also can they adjust to differing expectations in your two households. When you are clear in your limits and expectations of your kids, and when you don't use discipline, or the lack thereof, as a way to get back at your "ex," your kids will adjust to two disparate systems. "At Mom's house we go to bed late, but at Dad's we go to bed early."

■ ■ ■

Feeling Good About Discipline
THE COUPLES' GUIDE

1. Couples are bound to disagree about parenting tactics.
2. You each have valuable contributions to make.
3. A united front is good for your marriage and good for your child.
4. To resolve differences:
    - Approach the issue with a spirit of cooperation.
    - Make a list of your parenting goals.
    - Compare and analyze your lists.
    - Cross off the goals that you have in common.
    - Focus on one area at a time.
    - Keep an open mind.
5. Divorced couples should remember that children prefer one system of discipline.
6. Divorced couples who are unwilling to communicate with each other should teach their child that even though you each have different ways of doing things, you both love him.

PART THREE

Thorny Problems

CHAPTER TEN

Froot Loops
How to Deal Effectively with Tantrums

Every family with preschoolers has its favorite tantrum tales. Sometimes parents exchange them like war stories: "The Tantrums I've Survived" or "Can You Top This One?" We're sure you have one or two under your belts, too.

Our family is no exception. Here is a sampling of the three worst that we can remember:

FROOT LOOPS IN RALPHS

Ralphs is our local grocery store. Susan took three-year-old Cherie on her weekly marketing trip as was her habit. They counted "the eggies" in the egg carton. They named all the different fruits and vegetables. They even called out the color of every item as they put it in the shopping cart. Susan liked to view each trip to the market as a teaching opportunity.

She always enjoyed these outings with Cherie, until, one day, they hit the cereal aisle. Need we say more? Cherie, having recently been indoctrinated by TV ads, insisted that she wanted Froot Loops and nothing else. Cheerios or corn flakes, even her old favorite, granola, wouldn't do. Susan, as you may guess, had vowed that sugary cereals would not enter her household. Here we had the makings of a tantrum.

In her most patient voice, Susan said, "I know you want Froot Loops, but I'm not buying that kind of cereal. You can pick from these other ones."

Cherie wouldn't accept that. From her initial whining, she worked herself into a veritable fit, yelling and screaming at the top of her lungs.

Susan was trapped. She could feel her face flush, she started to sweat, and her knees became weak. Believing that giving in to the tantrum was tantamount to suicide, she stuck to her guns. She tried fruit(loop)lessly to silence Cherie with shushing and dirty looks.

Curious shoppers peered down the aisle to see what all the commotion was about. Susan could see them muttering and shaking their heads. She was sure that everybody in the store judged her harshly. After all, what kind of mother would cause her child to cry like that? Finally, Susan, nearly in tears herself from embarrassment, abandoned her cart of groceries and fled the market, screaming child in tow.

LOCKED OUT

Early one morning, Susan escorted Cherie out to the driveway, where a carpool had arrived to whisk her off for a day at nursery school. After waving good-bye to Cherie, Susan, dressed to the nines in her nightgown, comfy old robe, and scruffy slippers, returned to the kitchen door and, much to her dismay, found herself locked out of the house. Two-year-old Aimee apparently had managed to slam the kitchen door closed behind her mom.

"What to do?" thought Susan. She peered through the window and could see the top of Aimee's head. Aimee was standing right next to the door. Susan tried to coax the two-year-old to turn the knob to let her in. But try as she might, Susan couldn't communicate to Aimee what she wanted her to do.

Now, Aimee was fine for about two or three minutes. She could hear her mommy. She could even see her mommy if she looked up. But suddenly she decided that she wanted to feel her mommy. There was no doubt about it. She *wanted* her mommy. What ensued, of course, was a rather lusty tantrum.

Susan could not calm down Aimee through the door. Trying to find another way, she ran around the house, checking all the windows. It was 8:00 A.M., and the house was locked up tight. Foolishly, we had not hidden a spare key in the garage. There didn't seem to be any way in. Susan was beginning to panic.

Finally, with great reluctance and many assurances to screaming Aimee that "Mommy will be right back," Susan fled to the next-door neighbor's house and called the police (it never occurred to her to call a locksmith), requesting that they please come over as soon as possible to help her break into her own house.

STUCK ON THE ROOF

One day, Mitch and Susan decided to fix the TV antenna on the roof, which was no easy task. Undaunted, they set up the ladder in an enclosed courtyard at the front of the house where the roof was the lowest, scaled the ladder, and shimmied over the pitched eaves roofed with Mexican-style adobe tile before reaching the level area where they could stand.

Two-and-a-half-year-old Aimee had been napping during their ascent. She awakened, perhaps from the sounds of their voices and crunching footsteps above. In a cranky state, she wandered around the house looking for someone to fill her bottle with milk. When she didn't find anyone, she started whining. Mitch and Susan could hear her and called for her to come outside.

Obediently, Aimee went out to the courtyard, but when she saw her parents on the roof, where she couldn't get to them, she began wailing.

Fine. Susan decided to get down from her perch to take care of the problem. Unfortunately, as soon as she reached the edge of the roof, she froze in terror. Never before had she been a victim of vertigo and a fear of heights. But there she was, unable to slide down the eaves toward the ladder.

As the courtyard was enclosed on three sides and open to the heavens above, when Aimee started screaming, her cries bounced off the walls and carried all the way down the street. Neighbors and friends rushed over from parts east and west to see what was going on. They came upon Susan sitting bug-eyed on the tiled eaves while Mitch tried to coax her down to the ladder toward their screaming daughter.

TANTRUMS ARE NORMAL

It may be of little comfort for you to know that tantrums are a normal part of your child's development. Hate them as you may, your child is likely to have several if not many during his preschool years. They may even be good for him. It's how you deal with them that's important.

Your child's first tantrum usually comes as a terrible shock. We experienced ours when Cherie was only fifteen months old. We had heard rumors of "the terrible twos" but were certain that either this would never hit our family, or if it did, it was months away. We were quite wrong. Cherie had her *it's-time-to-break-mom-and-dad-in* tantrum the moment she discovered the new and powerful word *no* when we tried to dissuade her from swallowing a giant pop-bead.

Actually, when it happened, we were still quite inexperienced. We were both in graduate school, and none of our close friends had children yet—in fact, we were the first to get married. We didn't know how to proceed.

In the early '70s the only authority for most parents was Dr. Benjamin Spock. We quickly turned to the section on tantrums in his book Baby and Child Care, but we found that he did not give us enough support. He wrote mildly about distracting the child and providing him with enough toys and free playtime to keep him out of trouble. He asked questions such as, "When [mother] has to interrupt his play to get him indoors or to meals, does she frustrate him directly, or get his mind on something pleasant?" This seemed to blame the parent, rather than address the issue of the developing child. And his advice didn't fit what we were experiencing with Cherie.

In fact, we were horrified at what had happened to our wonderful, beautiful baby. Because of our upset, Mitch decided to take Cherie to be evaluated by Rose Bromwich, one of his professors who specialized in early childhood development.

It was the best thing we ever did. Dr. Bromwich observed us as we played with our child for 15 minutes. In the midst of our time together, Cherie did perform on cue. She had a tantrum when Mitch tried to prevent her from eating dirt.

"What's wrong with her, Dr. Bromwich?" Susan asked. "She never did this before. What should we do?"

"Wrong with her?" the good professor replied, smiling warmly. "She's perfectly normal. A delightful child. Bright and alert. She just developing her own identity. She's becoming a separate person from you. You want this to happen. In fact, you should thank God that it has. She is beginning to grow up.

"Sometimes she will have tantrums when she doesn't get her way. And sometimes she'll do it as an attention-getting device. This is all absolutely normal. There's nothing to worry about."

We went home a bit mollified, but we didn't feel better the next time Cherie lapsed into tumultuous spasms of screaming. OK, we thought, so it's normal to have tantrums. But . . .

HOW DO YOU GET YOUR CHILD TO STOP?

Most of the time, your child engages in tantrums as a means of gaining attention. He may be angry that you have thwarted one of his desires, or he may be refusing to do what you ask of him. In either case, his cries are an attempt to manipulate you into doing what he wants. He figures if he keeps it up long enough you will cave in, since you can't stand to see him in such a state.

Our friend Mindy and her daughter Angela were locked in this sort of battle (see Chapter 1) when Angela wanted to view a different videotape that the one her mother brought home. Mindy was on the verge of allowing her daughter's violent reaction to manipulate her into going back to the video store to exchange the tape.

As long as you have determined that your child is not in any kind of danger of pain, and recognize that the tantrum is his manipulative cry for attention, the obvious question is, How can you get the behavior to stop? The answer: Don't reinforce the tantrum. Simply put, that means ignore the tantrum. We had encouraged Mindy to leave the room with us when her daughter was having her fit. We did not want to reinforce Angela's behavior with our presence or reaction.

In order to stop the tantrum:

- Don't respond to it.
- Don't yell at your child.
- Don't try to talk him out of it.
- Don't make eye contact.
- Don't let him see that his behavior is getting to you.

Ignoring the tantrum, of course, is more difficult to do than it sounds, but we'll get to suggestions that can help you accomplish this feat of parental derring-do shortly.

If you don't ignore the tantrum, then you may continue to reinforce the tantrum behavior. Indeed, your preschooler may carry on with even more vigor and rage. This situation happened to John, one of Mitch's clients. John's oldest son, Kenny, was capable of endless tantrums and outrageous behavior. At four years old, Kenny had become a little tyrant in his home.

Here was the problem: John lived in an apartment building, and every time Kenny screamed and carried on, John's neighbor in the adjacent apartment, Frank, would bang on the wall. Frank never failed to let John know how unhappy he was with Kenny's crying. "Can't you get that kid to shut up?" he groused.

John felt bad about this, but didn't know what to do. Without really thinking about it, he began to give in to Kenny's demands just to keep him quiet. As you can surmise from our previous discussion, John's approach took care of the immediate problem but, in general, made matters worse. Kenny even began throwing things and hitting his little brother when he didn't get his way.

By the time he consulted Mitch, John was a wreck. Mitch talked to him about limit setting, consistent consequence, and follow-through as a way to contain Kenny's obnoxious behavior. Mitch suggested that John begin by allowing Kenny to cry it out when he was having his next tantrum. John wasn't keen on that idea. "After all," he explained, "we got into this mess because Frank objected to Kenny's crying in the first place."

Mitch's question to John: "Does Frank pay your rent?"

"Why, no. Of course not."

"Then why should you let him dictate what you do in the privacy of your own apartment? You may have to let Kenny cry in order to take care of his behavior problems. If your neighbors don't like it, that's their affair. It shouldn't concern you. Your first priority is to appropriately parent your son, who is having a very hard time right now. Perhaps you can explain that to Frank. He may be more sympathetic if he understands what is going on."

Together they devised a plan to help extinguish Kenny's violent behavior. You, too, can follow these suggestions when your child loses control of himself.

HOW TO CURB THE TANTRUM

1. *Separate yourself physically from the child.* Put him in his room or in the kitchen while you stay in the living room. Whatever you do, distance yourself. He will do anything for your attention. If you stay in the same room with him, somehow you will manage to make eye contact, which, as you know, is very reinforcing. Or he may sense you're upset by detecting the tension in your body. Keep your distance.

2. *Don't try to reason with the child.* When your preschooler gets carried away by her own anger, there is no point in trying to discuss with her the pros and cons of your opposing position. She can't hear you, and, in truth, you just want her to stop. You can say, "When you're finished screaming, you can come into the living room and *with your words* tell me what's bothering you." You can't deal with her when she's

screaming, so don't even try. Stick to your commitment.

3. *Be persistent and creative.* Never one to make things easy on us, Cherie sometimes refused to stay in her room throughout the course of her tantrum. She would burst out of her room, screaming like a banshee. We escorted her right back, reiterating the words, "When you're finished screaming, we'll be happy to talk to you about your problem." You may have to repeat this several times, broken-record style, before your child gets the message.

On several occasions, we found it necessary to lock ourselves into our own room. Cherie sat out in the hallway, wailing at our closed door. Again, we called to her through the door, "When you stop crying and are ready to talk about it, we'll come out."

One of our friends found it necessary to eject her daughter from the house whenever she had a tantrum. About once a week, Michelle could be found wandering up and down the fenced driveway, stamping her feet and screaming her head off. The neighbors weren't very happy about it, but that's what it took.

4. *Let him cry it out.* This is the toughest part! You must be consistent. If you give into the tantrum once, you may prolong the misery for all of you. The next time your child has a tantrum, he'll feel that if he just keeps at it long enough, you will submit to his desires. Each time that you cave in, you reinforce the tantrum, and the next tantrum will be worse. We discuss the pitfalls of such *intermittent-reinforcement schedules* in Chapter 6.

Remember, you are not hurting your preschooler by letting him cry. Instead, you are teaching him that you are unwilling to go along with every little desire. You are in charge, and you won't be manipulated. This message becomes more and more important as he grows older—especially when he nears adolescence.

5. *Use positive reinforcement.* Once your preschooler has

calmed down, praise her to the skies for having explained her problem in her words. You can say, "I like when you talk to me. I can really listen to you when you're not screaming. Let's see if we can work this out." By paying attention to the good things that she does, you help eliminate those activities that you feel are destructive. (See Chapter 7 on positive reinforcement.)

6. *Use mirroring*. Mirroring is a way of validating your child's feelings without necessarily giving in to what she wants. Susan used mirroring (unfortunately to little avail) in the supermarket when she said to Cherie, "I understand that you want Froot Loops . . ." It didn't work at that point because Cherie had the upper hand: She hadn't gotten to the talking stage yet.

Mirroring is most effective once your preschooler has calmed down. You can say, "You must have been pretty upset that I wouldn't let you pick all of Mrs. Mulligan's flowers, but that's just not OK. Let's ask her if she'll allow us to pick just one." In this way, you are letting your child know that you recognize her feelings even if you don't permit her to have her own way. She is valued, but you are in charge.

WHAT IF YOU'RE AT THE SUPERMARKET?

Children have a great way of finding your weak spot and then pouncing on it. If they sense that you're concerned about appearances, they may decide to throw a fit when you're out at a restaurant, at your parents' home, with friends, or in the supermarket. In so doing, they hope that you'll have to give into them because it's too embarrassing for you to let them cry it out in public.

What should you do if your preschooler persistently takes advantage of your vulnerabilities and flies out of control in a public place? In his book *How to Stop the Battle with Your*

Child, psychologist Don Fleming makes some valuable suggestions about what to do in the supermarket. We quote them for you here, with appropriate commentary:

"*The First Step*: Tell your child the rules ahead of time." That means informing him that you want him to behave by staying close to you and listening when you ask him to stop a particular behavior. You may let him ask for one item at the market. Let him decide which one, making sure that it's within the limits you've set in advance. "If you're conscious of nutrition, allow him to have some sugarless gum or something similar which will be agreeable to him." He can choose the flavor.

"*The Second Step*: Tell him even if you're in line with all of your groceries, if he can't control himself you will put the basket aside, take him to the car, and make him sit in the car for five minutes. (You should stand outside the car, looking away from him in order not to give any attention to your child.)" This tactic creates the same sort of isolation that you would produce if you were at home and could send your son to his room to cry it out. After five minutes, if he calms down, you can try going back into the market again.

"*The Third Step*: If you try a second time and he persists in being uncooperative, you must be willing to leave the food (not a popular tactic with grocery managers, incidentally!), go home, and give him an immediate consequence." This may seem as if it's hurting you more than it is him, since you've been unsuccessful in completing your shopping trip. But in truth, you will be demonstrating that it is so important for your child to gain control over his behavior that you are willing to sacrifice a trip to the market to gain that end.

"*The Fourth Step* is to prepare him to try again the next time you go to the market." Dr. Fleming suggests using positive statements such as "I know you can do it. Do you want to try again?" Be prepared, however, for the eventuality that your preschooler may blow it once more. If he does, you must remove him again and increase the consequence at home. You need not get angry. "Simply say to him, 'I guess you weren't ready.'"

These suggestions can go a long way in helping you to curb your child's tantrums at the market. They're also applicable when you're out shopping at other locations, dining at a restaurant, or visiting friends or relatives. You do have to commit, however, to taking charge and perhaps cutting a visit short when the screaming begins. If possible, inform your friends and relatives in advance that Jeffrey is working on a behavior problem and that you may need to leave early if he can't handle himself properly. Explain your tactics so they'll know that it's nothing personal.

A WORD ABOUT LETTING HIM CRY IT OUT

Our friend Mindy feared that if she gave Angela free rein in crying, she would in some way damage her child emotionally. Generally this is not true. Your firm, consistent, and reasonable approach during a tantrum teaches your child that you care enough about her to set limits about her behavior. It makes her feel safe to know that you are in charge, even if she objects to it. Eventually Angela exhausted herself and stopped crying. The trick for Mindy was to be able to tolerate the screaming and feel good about herself as a parent at the same time.

Another friend, Barbara, heard stories that her son's tantrums would escalate to dangerous proportions if she left him alone to cry. She was afraid that he would bang his head on the floor or hold his breath until he passed out.

In truth, behavior as severe as this is very rare. It hurts to hit yourself in the head repeatedly. No child is going to keep this up for long. If, however, you find that you have a tough youngster on your hands, you can say, "It's OK for you to have a tantrum, but I'm not going to allow you to hurt yourself or others." You can put a pillow under his head (so long as his breathing is unimpaired) or hold his arms at his sides if he is flailing out at others.

Breath-holding is scary to witness. It may look to you as if your child is going to die. But remember, this extreme form of manipulation has a way of working itself out. If, indeed, your child insists on holding his breath until he becomes blue in the face and passes out, nature has a way of taking care of things. Once he has fainted, his autonomic nervous system take over, and he will begin breathing involuntarily. Nevertheless, this is a frightening tactic. Let's hope you have curbed your child's tantrums before they ever reach this point. If not, it would be wise to seek the assistance of a qualified child counselor.

WATCH YOUR MIXED MESSAGES

One of Mitch's clients had a lot of trouble with her daughter's tantrums. Nancy discussed tantrum strategies in Mitch's office and then followed the suggestions at home with Marla. Yet her three-year-old continued to rage on and on.

Mitch decided to have a closer look. He asked Nancy to bring Marla to the next session so that he could diagnose what in the communications between mother and daughter was encouraging the tantrums to persist with such potency.

As soon as Marla and Nancy entered the room, Mitch could see that he had his work cut out for him. Marla was a bright, cute, curious, and mischievous little girl. She was into everything. Nancy, on the other hand, was controlling and rigid.

She didn't want Marla to touch anything in the office since she feared her daughter would disturb the décor or break something. She held onto Marla's hand tightly.

Almost as soon as the session started, mother and daughter got into a power struggle over a little vase on a low table. Marla wanted to play with it, and Nancy wouldn't let her.

"I want it, I want it," said Marla.

"I'm sorry, you can't play with this vase. It belongs to Dr. Golant, and I'm afraid you'll break it," her mother replied, holding the piece of pottery up in the air.

"But I want it," Marla began crying.

Nancy took the vase and put it up on a shelf where Marla couldn't reach it.

Thus provoked, Marla twisted herself away from her mother's grasp, threw herself on the floor, and began kicking and screaming. After a few minutes of trying to calm down her daughter herself, Nancy turned to Mitch for help.

Although it took most of the rest of the session for Marla to gain control of her rage, Mitch was pleased. He had the answer that he was looking for.

In the next session, Nancy came alone to discuss her difficulties with her daughter's behavior. She began by complaining about how discouraging she was finding the task of child-rearing.

Mitch heard her out but then posed a question. "Did you notice," he said, "that you were smiling while Marla was having her tantrum?"

That was rather a shock to Nancy. "Smiling? Was I really?"

"Yes. Why do you suppose you were doing that? What would make you respond in that way?"

So began some weeks of soul searching on Nancy's part. When she dug deep into her past, she remembered how her parents had dealt with her own tantrums when she was a child. They wouldn't let her have them. Her mother, of the old, strict European school of child-rearing, would say, "So, if you're going to cry, I'm going to give you something to cry about," and then spank her on the rear when Nancy had a tantrum.

When Nancy recalled these incidents, she realized that on some unconscious level, she was really happy that her daughter had the freedom to express her anger. The tantrums actually made Nancy giggle inside. She could experience the full range of expression that was denied to her as a child. "Look," she was saying to herself, "I'm letting Marla do what I couldn't do. Isn't it great?"

It was great, except that it was reinforcing Marla's tantrums. On the one hand Nancy was secretly happy that Marla was having a tantrum, but on the other Nancy was secretly jealous and overtly angry that her daughter got to do something that she never had permission to do. No wonder Nancy was unsuccessful. She was sending her child very confusing messages. She wasn't fully committed to controlling the behavior, and Marla was smart enough to pick that up.

Once Nancy recognized and owned up to her part in this little conspiracy, she was able to suppress her smile when her daughter acted out. That made controlling Marla's tantrums a lot easier.

Incidents such as these demonstrate how complicated child-rearing really is. So many factors come into play. Sometimes a simple formula about what to do just doesn't work because you have your own unresolved issues that creep into your interactions with your child. This can't be helped. You are human and subject to emotions and frailties as are the rest of us. But what you can achieve is to become aware of the part that you play in the equation, as Nancy did, and then use that self-awareness to help your child grow. Nobody ever said that child-rearing is easy. It's not! But the rewards are wonderful.

■ ■ ■

Feeling Good About Discipline
GUIDE TO TANTRUMS

1. Tantrums are a normal part of development.
2. Don't reinforce the behavior. Ignore it:
   - Separate yourself physically from your child.
   - Don't try to reason with him.
   - Be persistent and creative.
   - Let him cry it out.
   - Use positive reinforcement when he explains his problems in his own words.
   - Use mirroring to validate his feelings.
3. If you're at the supermarket, and a tantrum occurs:
   - Tell your child the rules in advance.
   - Tell him you'll both leave if he can't control himself.
   - Follow through on your promise.
   - If he can't handle it, go home and try again the next time.
4. Watch for mixed messages and unconscious problems that creep in from your own childhood.

CHAPTER ELEVEN

What About Lying?

FOUR-YEAR-OLD STEVEN had received a new truck from his parents. Accidentally, the truck fell into his trash can, and later no one could find it. Steven didn't have a ready explanation for the loss of his new toy, so he developed a story that went something like this: "I was playing with my truck outside when this boy came over. He asked me if he could play with me, and I said, OK. So he played for a while, and then he borrowed the truck and went home with it."

It was a plausible enough story, but Steven couldn't supply any of the details. Who was the boy? Where did he live? Was he with his mom? None of the specifics were forthcoming. And Steven's parents were at a loss to find a way to get the new truck back.

That evening, when Steven was fast asleep, his mom, Barbara, went to dump the trash. It was then that she discovered the truck in Steven's trash can. Maybe he threw it away and didn't want to tell us, she thought. This upset her very much. It wasn't the first time her son had made up stories. Barbara came to Mitch to deal with Steven's lying. She wanted her son to stop.

PRESCHOOLERS DON'T LIE

Conscious lying doesn't occur until the age of about seven years old, according to Dr. Lawrence Kohlberg, a psychologist who has researched the development of a child's sense of morals. You may find this a shocking statement, but by and large it's true. That's not to say that, by adult standards, preschoolers are absolutely honest all of the time either, because they're not. Preschoolers see the world as revolving around themselves. Children at this age find that they can manipulate words, images, and ideas in their minds. If they can visualize a notion in their heads, then they believe that it must be true. It's part of their natural egocentrism. They tell stories. So how can you square both of these conflicting ideas? It takes a little understanding of child development to do so.

Storytelling is a part of your preschooler's development. Parents often have problems with storytelling because they judge the kids' behavior by adult standards. What may be appropriate for you as an adult may not be appropriate for your child. When an adult fabricates, usually you can interpret it as a willful act. He knows right from wrong. He knows what has happened and tells an untruth to protect himself or to get the better of you. He is lying.

For preschoolers, on the other hand, fabrication or storytelling is a form of imaginative play. It's just one stage of their development. Some kids concoct elaborate stories to explain an incident. They may do so to make themselves look bigger in the eyes of parents or friends, or they may simply take pleasure in playing with ideas and words. As we explained in Chapter 2, preschoolers don't have a clear sense of right and wrong or rules.

There was a *Sesame Street* sequence years ago that illustrates this point. It was a story of a little girl who spilled her milk at the table. Her mom came in, predictably angry, and asked what had happened to the milk. The girl made up all sorts of tales. One was the possibility that her little brother's ball had knocked over the glass. Another was the tale that a herd of elephants had stomped through the kitchen and shaken the table to such a degree that the milk sloshed out of the glass. It's a ridiculous story, and it used to make our kids giggle. But it's absolutely accurate in its intent. That's what preschoolers do.

Sometimes it's clear to you when your child is making up tall tales. For example, if Steven had said, "I was playing outside, and there was this big hole. Then the rain came, and the hole filled up with water, and the truck floated away to the ocean," or "I was playing by Fido's bowl, and Fido was hungry so he ate the truck," then his parents would have recognized the imaginative nature of his response. But since his story about the boy had such a ring of truth to it, they interpreted that he had made up the falsehood on purpose.

On the other hand, if your seven-year-old fills up his straw with milk, blows it all over the face of his three-year-old sister, pretending to "slash" her throat with his straw (as one of Mitch's clients did) and says, "But Mom, we were just playing," you can bet that there may be a little lying going on. But your seven-year-old is at the stage where he can distinguish right from wrong.

HOW DO YOU DEAL WITH YOUR CHILD'S TALL TALES?

If your preschooler is creating some real whoppers, don't get upset and don't punish him. Here's what you can do:

1. *Don't call him a liar.* This is most important. Your preschooler's stories should not be looked upon as lies. His stories are a way for him to adapt to his world. He is learn-

ing to use words not only as a way of communicating but as a means to take charge of his own life.

If you label John a liar, you may reinforce behavior you'd like him to stop. Labeling of any kind stereotypes your children. It narrows your view of them and their view of themselves. He may find that these stories get him a lot of attention—even if it's negative. This may prompt John to create more and more elaborate tales, for the sake of that attention. As he gets older and understands what lying really means, he may feel obligated to live up to your negative view of him, which will have profound effects on his self-esteem.

So when your child tells tall tales, realized that he is looking for a way to control his world and be successful.

2. *Go along in the same spirit.* If Felicia tells you that her pets are all wet because it's raining cats and dogs, you can say, "What a wonderful story you've just told me! What is it like when it rains cats and dogs?"

She may reply, "They all come falling out of the sky, and they bring the water with them, and they land in the backyard in a big pile. And then they splash around and play with each other."

You could inject a bit of "reality" by suggesting, "Isn't it also possible that you made Prince and Duke all wet with the hose?"

She may agree with you, or she may say, "I took Prince's water bowl and splashed him with it. He looked so hot. And then Duke wanted to play, too, so I got him wet also. They sure look funny when they're wet!"

3. *Appreciate the creativity of the story.* Flexible thinking is another way of looking at storytelling at this age. In this kind of thought process, your child applies a known entity to a new situation. For example, he figures out how to use the cardboard core of a paper-towel roll as a megaphone, a telephone, or a spyglass. Flexible thinking is one of the skills used to identify gifted children.

If you force your preschooler into responding to his world in an adult way, you may be asking him to give up some of the wonders of childhood. As long as it hurts no one, what's the harm in his doing a little creative storytelling? When he is old enough, he will eventually grasp the concept of wrong and right. For now, he's just playing.

You can appreciate your child's flexible thinking by recognizing its importance in the creative process. Instead of saying, "That's stupid. No one would believe a story like that," you can say, "Wow! How interesting. How did you ever think up an idea like that?"

WHAT IF YOUR CHILD *REALLY* LIES?

There are rare exceptions to our statement that preschoolers don't lie. Some do. At this developmental stage, however, children who lie consciously do so as a way of protecting themselves from anticipated hurt.

More than anything, your preschooler wants your approval and love. He may try to enhance your view of him by embellishing the truth. For your child, it becomes an issue of trust. If he feels inadequate in your eyes, he may not trust that you love him just the way he is. It's a matter of trust for you, as well. You would like to believe that what he has to say is the truth.

Unfortunately, some parents set up an environment in which the truth isn't acceptable. That is, they have an ideal image of what they want their children to be like, and they don't want to hear anything that doesn't support this image.

Mitch encountered this situation in his practice. Timmy wanted to please his parents, so he told them a tale about how the cat got away. It involved an elaborate scheme in which Timmy figures as the thwarted hero. His father responded negatively. "That can't be true," he said. "You always lie. You let the cat run away. How could you do such a thing and then tell me these stories! You're really going to get it!" Rather than feeling better about himself, Timmy felt diminished and misunderstood. As often happens in such a situation, the child withdrew.

The next time something bad happened, Timmy kept silent. He didn't tell his parents that he spilled grape juice all over his new shirt. When the shirt was discovered scrunched up in a tiny ball under Timmy's bed, a week later, his father was even angrier. He said, "How come you didn't tell me? You always lie."

This difficult attitude set up a painful double-bind for the child. He can't win either way he goes. If he tells the truth (that he let the cat out), he will get punished. If he lies, by embellishing the story, he will also get punished. He loses hope of ever gaining his parents' love and approval.

If you recognize your own family dynamics in this situation, your awareness will help to rectify the situation. All parents and children have encountered the problem. It makes you neither good nor bad as a parent. It helps you to become aware of your high expectations and to perhaps alter those expectations to make them more reasonable. A four-year-old, after all, is bound to misbehave once in a while. Too bad it had to be your pet cat or his new shirt.

To break this kind of cycle may take some discipline on your part, especially if you have a very strong sense of morality. Remember, your preschooler's stories are just that—fiction, and nothing more. The key is to begin to have a conversation about the tale with your child. In this case, Mitch encouraged Timmy's dad to explore the fantasy with his son the next time he came up with a fanciful explanation. He said, "Isn't it fun to make up stories? It's so nice to have a mind that can see pictures and use words."

The use of words like *always* (as in, "You always lie.") and *never* are a form of labeling that exacerbates the potential for lying as well. They don't allow for the possibility of change. Timmy's parents needed to be reminded that everyone's feelings are in a constant state of flux. Using generalities such as *always* and *never* can prevent their son from correcting his behavior. Such expressions led Timmy to believe that there was no hope for redemption, which only intensified his sense of unworthiness.

When Timmy's dad was able to incorporate some of Mitch's suggestions, he could let go of his unrealistic expectations of his son. This helped to defuse the conflict and allowed Timmy space to do what a four-year-old does naturally—play.

MORE SERIOUS SITUATIONS

When the consequence does not fit the crime, there is a greater likelihood for abuse and lying (see Chapter 5). Abuse is often a parental response to frustration. When you are frustrated, you are less apt to take the time to deal with the situation in a reasoned manner and come up with a logical consequence. You may feel personally threatened by your child's behavior. Most parents certainly don't want to abuse their children, but they may do so unconsciously.

Sadly, some young children who tell deliberate lies have been subjected to an inordinate amount of physical and emotional abuse, neglect, and personal trauma. Lying becomes a coping mechanism to delay imminent pain. Mitch had a particularly difficult case that illustrates this point. He learned from this family that abused preschoolers can lie as a way of protecting themselves.

Sally and Jim came to Mitch because they were having trouble with their three-and-a-half-year-old, Phillip. It seemed that whenever Phillip misbehaved, he lied to cover up.

Mitch encouraged Sally and Jim to talk with their son about how much fun it is to imagine stories. Although they tried this approach, it didn't work. Phillip continued to cover up after himself.

Mitch was perplexed by the lack of progress. He thought that maybe the theory was wrong—perhaps preschoolers do lie in certain situations. Then it occurred to him that he hadn't pursued in detail what consequences Sally and Jim used with their son when he misbehaved.

With some gentle probing, he discovered that Jim threatened his little boy while he was yelling at him. He placed a belt on the table in front of his son as he questioned him. And, in truth, he did hit the boy with the belt. Phillip had learned that lying was a way to delay punishment.

When the full story came out, Mitch referred this family to the appropriate child-protective-services agency, as required by state law. Mitch, the protective-services caseworker, and the family worked out a system of monitoring to prevent a continuation of the abuse.

In therapy, Phillip began to improve markedly. It had become clear that the lying was only a symptom of a deeper disturbance in the family. Once the abuse abated, Mitch worked with the family on issues of trust. Phillip had to learn to trust that his parents weren't going to hurt him anymore. This took a long time. Because of the difficulties with intermittent reinforcement (see Chapter 6), Phillip tested his parents often. Although at times, Sally and Jim were at wits' end, Mitch was eventually able to bring the family closer together. They all understood what mistakes had been made and in what direction the work needed to take them.

Indeed, sometimes "problem" children reflect serious marital difficulties between their parents. Not all cases are so severe. Conversely, not all severe cases are as successful. Sometimes parents don't want to hear that they could be doing something wrong and decide to terminate the therapy abruptly. They view their child's acting out as the problem, rather than as a symptom of dysfunction with the family system.

Although Sally and Jim's is an extreme case, one can empathize with their frustration. Whacking a child certainly provides an easy out. Yet what makes humans so special is their ability to reason and use language. Any discipline needs to use and ultimately develop reasoning and language capacities in our children. How often do we tell our children, "Don't hit. Use your words." Yet if we are in the habit of using physical punishment ourselves, we reinforce the opposite response. Indeed, our physical threat or violence certainly work against our children's ability to settle their own conflicts without resorting to violence as well.

If you are reading this and recognize negative family disturbances as acted out by your preschooler, you should consider seeking professional help and counseling. If your preschooler is actually lying to protect himself, his behavior is a red flag signaling that something is amiss in the family. The problem may not lie so much with the child as with the other members of your household. These problems are best attended to as soon as possible.

Limit setting with love and appropriate logical consequences, coupled with your knowledge of child development, will increase the feelings of closeness in your family and help you to deal with the problem of lying. Based on years of research, our suggestions become part of an overall and ongoing process to make loving and effective discipline an integral part of your family dynamics.

■ ■ ■

Feeling Good About Discipline
GUIDE TO LYING

1. Preschoolers don't lie, they tell stories.
2. These stories are your child's way of manipulating words and ideas to have some control over his world.
3. These stories are a form of imaginative play.
4. To deal with tall tales:
   - Don't label your child or call him a liar.
   - Go along in the same spirit.
   - Appreciate the creativity of the story.
5. If your child *really* lies, she may be asking for more approval. Have a conversation with her about her stories.
6. Chronic lying may be a sign of abuse. Seek family counseling.

CHAPTER TWELVE

Refereeing Sibling Arguments

How Everyone Can Win

THIS CHAPTER was our children's idea. After we had finished preparing a suggested outline for this book and before we turned it over to our publisher, we thought it wise to pass the table of contents in front of the girls' noses for their feedback.

"This looks great," said our then eighteen-year-old, Cherie. "But if this book is going to be about discipline, why doesn't it have anything in it on sibling rivalry? We had our worst time over those kinds of fights."

"Yeah," chimed in fifteen-year-old Aimee. "If you want to really help people, you should give them advice about what to do when their kids don't get along. I used to *hate* it when Cherie wouldn't let me play with her friend Laura and their Barbies."

"Or when Aim took my markers and left the caps off so they all dried out. I could have *killed* her."

Great idea, kids. They were glowering at each other already, poised to have at it again. It was amazing how those hurts, inflicted so long ago, still continued to ache. Yes, a chapter on sibling rivalry was in order since many discipline problems arise from sibling conflicts. We needed to cover how to get at the roots of the problem to help defuse the hostility before it becomes explosive as well as how to referee fights so that everyone wins—perhaps even ease the hostility before it begins. The girls were absolutely right.

RELIVING YOUR OWN PAST

While our kids had the right idea, it became abundantly clear to Susan, as the work progressed, that this was the most difficult chapter for her to write. We went through multiple revisions and still she could not get it right. After thinking about the writing process, Susan realized that this segment was giving her the most trouble because she had many unresolved issues with her own sister, who was a scant fourteen months older than she. Although she and her sibling had become friends over the years, there was still a residue of jealousy and tension between them. These unresolved, unconscious feelings had a way of blocking her writing process.

Mitch, on the other hand, had had an entirely different experience. His brother was nearly ten years older than he was. During Mitch's childhood, his brother had become a comfort, a substitute parent, and an ally in a family that was racked with marital discord. Mitch had no difficulty in the sibling arena.

We bring this point up because over the years we have come to realize that we relive with our children every step of our own development. When they are infants, our feelings of helplessness are rekindled; when they are preschoolers, their struggles bring up specters of our own attempts to master the world around us; when they are preadolescents, we rock and roll with their hormonal swings and our memories of these tumultuous times. In effect, we grow up again with our children. As parents, we cannot be separated from our own past.

Indeed, while we discussed this chapter with our daughters, Cherie suggested including material on birth order. She felt that since we were both younger children in households with two kids, we could never fully appreciate her pain as a "displaced" older sibling. Perhaps she was right. We certainly tried, but hers was not an experience that either of us could identify with completely since we had not lived through it ourselves. We are all products of our own experience.

As you go through this chapter, it's important to bear in mind how your own experience growing up in your parents' household colors your reactions and responses to your children's squabbles. In answering the following questions, see what memories and images from your own childhood are evoked and how these can apply to situations today. We suggest writing your answers on a separate piece of paper so that you have something concrete to work with.

■ ■ ■

Feeling Good About Discipline
PARENT/SIBLING CHECKLIST

1. Were you first, second, or third in birth order?
2. Did your position in the family empower you relative to your older and/or younger sibling(s)?
3. Is there a similarity in power structure with your children, and if so, how?
4. Did you take on the role of victim?
5. Were you a bully?

6. Do you see any of your children as a victim or bully?
7. Were you the smart/beautiful/intelligent child or the athletic/artistic/stupid one?
8. Were you cast in the role of caretaker?
9. Do you tend to categorize your own children in a similar way?
10. How did your parents respond to sibling fights?
11. Did they take sides, and was there favoritism?
12. Did you feel you were treated fairly or unfairly?
13. Today do you feel the urge to take sides in refereeing family arguments, and if so, how and with whom?
14. Have you been able to resolve conflicts with your sibling(s) today?
15. How do your experiences as a sister or brother affect the way you treat your own children?

The reliving of our past can take many forms. In our job as parents, we may have tried to compensate for mistakes made in our childhood homes. Sometimes in our haste to make things better, we can overcompensate or act inappropriately without even realizing it. For example, you may secretly encourage your youngest to be a bully because, as the "baby" in your own family, you were always cast in the role of a victim. You take forbidden pleasure in her getting the best of her older brother because you could never stand up to your older brother when you were her age.

If we haven't considered our children in light of our own past before, we may also unconsciously repeat patterns established by our parents. If your parents punished you severely for fighting with your sister, you may feel the urge to do the same when your brood is not getting along, even though rationally you know that punishment only promotes resentment.

The impact of our own childhood on our current child-rearing practices is vast and multifaceted. In general, however, we could say that our own experiences affect

- how much and in what way we empathize with our children
- the methods and approach that we use for discipline.

The personal information that you unearth from answering the questions we pose in the checklist may be as significant in helping to resolve family conflicts as any other piece of learned advice that we can share with you. If you can become aware of the way you were treated, then you have the opportunity to do things differently from your parents in your own family. Insights into your own past can help change the way that you discipline your children.

WHY DO YOUR CHILDREN FIGHT WITH EACH OTHER, ANYWAY?

It is impossible to raise children without some measure of sibling rivalry and conflict. In fact, when our second daughter was born, somehow it seemed as if our house was loaded with children. We felt that our parenting task had increased geometrically and not just arithmetically. It was as if one plus one equals four.

For some parents, as was our good luck, the care of the second baby (as long as she is healthy) is much easier than the first. We are well seasoned as mommy and daddy and know what to expect and how to proceed. Formula is no longer an incalculable mystery, nor baby baths an excursion into dangerous waters. Baby's first sniffle is not the signal to call the paramedics for emergency resuscitation. Yes, the physical part of caring for a second child seems simple when you are more confident of yourself as a parent.

But the interrelations among the family members are utterly more complicated. You cope with the relationship between mom and the baby, dad and the baby, older sibling and the baby, mom with older sibling and the baby, dad with older sibling and the baby. Mom with dad and grandpa and the baby. . . . The permutations are almost limitless.

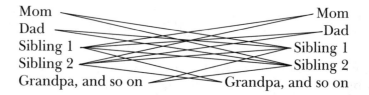

In families with three or more children, the complications increase exponentially. The older siblings form alliances and gang up on the younger ones, or it can be the girls against the boys. The younger kids may be stigmatized as "tagalongs." The techniques that we share later in this chapter apply for all sibling situations, be they in family of two kids or twelve kids. In addition, fair family meetings are crucial for opening communication and maintaining peace in such larger households.

Family relationships (especially when a new baby enters the home) can be fraught with difficulties. Cherie, having been our only child for nearly four years and our parents' first geographically available grandchild, was the apple of everyone's eye. After years of our exclusive attention, predictably she did not take to her little sister very well. This is not to say that she didn't try at least to impress us with the great demonstrations of affection that she thought we expected. There were the obligatory hugs (a little too tight) and kisses (a little too hard), coupled with patently false statements such as "I love my new baby sister sooooo much," uttered with a little too much vehemence between clenched teeth. The fact was, Cherie loved her new sister, all right— if allowed to have her way, she probably would have loved Aimee almost to death.

We had thought, innocently enough, that since Cherie had reached the ripe old age of three and three-quarters, was happy in her nursery school, and had friends and a life of her own, the arrival of her sibling would not create a disturbance in her life. Wrong again. Cherie was miserable. She interpreted any time that we spent with Aimee as an affront and a deep rejection.

This, of course, is quite normal and to be expected. After all, most of us would feel terribly displaced if we experienced ourselves as being supplanted by a young interloper in the hearts of our most cherished loved ones. Authors and parenting educators Adele Faber and Elaine Mazlish give an excellent demonstration of how this works in their book *Siblings Without Rivalry*:

> Imagine that your spouse puts an arm around you and says, "Honey, I love you so much, and you're so wonderful that I've decided to have another wife just like you. . . . When the new wife finally arrives, you see that she is very young and kind of cute. When the three of you are out together, people say hello to you politely, but exclaim ecstatically over the newcomer. . . . The new wife needs clothing. Your husband goes into your closet, takes some of your sweaters and pants and gives them to her. . . . One day you find your husband and the new wife lying on the bed together. He's tickling her and she's giggling. . . .

Your normal response to this kind of deep insult is hurt, anger, and the wish for revenge. Why would you expect your child to react any differently? In truth, it's painful to be an older sibling. Children express their anger and pain in a variety of ways:

- Monica teases Rebecca to distraction.
- Tony pops Ian on the head every chance he gets.
- Jeremy won't share any of his possessions with Samantha.
- Jill won't even let Eric into her room.

And it's painful to be a younger sibling as well. One may have to put up with endless put-downs, rejections, and taunts. Some children may take on the role of victim as a result of this bullying, while others fight back when enraged. This situation occurred in Susan's childhood home. Susan's older sister was a teaser who never tired of provoking her as a way to get attention. When Susan had just about all she could take, she fought back by hitting, pinching, or otherwise swatting away the gadfly that was bothering her. "Mommy, Susie hit me," was her sister's lament. Guess who got punished?

While you would fantasize your children loving each other and getting along, it's important to recognize that jealousy is a normal part of family dynamics. *Your children are bound to feel jealous of one another.* Jealousy can be painful, but it is not a sin. It's a human emotion that your child may need to express.

The scene that exemplifies our children's jealousy occurred one afternoon when both girls were out in the backyard playing. It seemed to Susan that it was quiet for hours, although in actuality only fifteen minutes had passed without a fight breaking out. Susan was curious to discover what entertained our kids to such an extent that they kept the peace for so long.

What she observed, peeking through a window, made her laugh out loud. There was four-year-old Aimee, bedecked in Cherie's hat and shoes, pushing the stroller with all her might around the patio. And who should be playing baby in the stroller? Why her seven-year-old big sister, of course, waving a long-lost bottle, sucking her thumb, and gurgling mock baby noises like "Goo goo gaa gaa."

This crystallized for Susan the essence of sibling rivalry. Each child believed that the other had it better. Each one wished to be in the other's shoes. They were both deliriously happy in their fantasized role reversal.

USE FANTASY PLAY TO HELP YOUR CHILDREN GET ALONG WITH EACH OTHER IN THE FIRST PLACE

Our children's fantasy play brings up an important point. Sibling rivalry and conflict can begin for some children the day the new baby is brought home. For others, it even begins before that. One of our friends complained that when she held her preschooler on her pregnant abdomen, she got a double whammy. The fetus was kicking from within, while her three-year-old was kicking from without. Ouch!

These conflicts are unavoidable but you can deal with them effectively by using your child's creative and fertile imagination. One way to engage your child's fantasy play is to make use of his regression at the birth of a sibling.

Regression means going back to an old way of doing things. Your preschooler may regress after a new sibling comes into the house. Your previously "grown up" older child can revert to bed-wetting, thumb sucking, tantrums, and even protestations of helplessness with the baby's arrival. Regression often occurs when your child is feeling insecure, under stress, or frightened.

Developmentally, your preschooler will go through many bursts of independence and clinginess. This is part of her learning to separate from you and become her own person. You can think of her like a yo-yo: She can go "around the world" but still she must come back, especially if it feels scary "out there." The farther out she steps on her own, the closer she must return, and the clingier she may become.

Since the birth of a sibling is perceived as a grave threat to her security, your preschooler may return to an old state of being where she felt safe at this difficult time in her life. Remember, acting grown-up is a state of mind and not a chronological age.

Regression can be frustrating. You may resent the reappearance of the babyish behavior in your preschooler, when she was already competent in caring for many of her own physical needs herself. In an effort to have her change, you may feel tempted to yell at Melissa to "Act her age" or "Stop being a baby" or to punish her for giving you a hard time. In truth, you have your hands full with one infant and are not thrilled by the prospect of your preschooler's reverting to immature, more clingy behavior. Your anger is a natural response.

But although it may be a pain in the neck for you, your preschooler's regression is not in and of itself bad, as we used to believe. In fact, paradoxical as it may seem, Melissa's return to thumb sucking serves as a way for her to grow up. The regression is a sign that is telling you she has something important to deal with and may need your help. That's why it feels as if a new baby adds more than one person to the household.

Sometimes you have to allow your preschooler to act younger in order to help her grow up. How can you use your child's regression to help her deal with her jealousy? Here are some suggestions that may assist you:

1. *Watch what you say.* Difficult as it may feel to you, resist your temptation to push Jonathan away with "You're older now. You should know better than that" when he comes to you after wetting his pants. Do not ridicule him for backsliding. This will reinforce his behavior and can encourage it to persist. His toilet-training habits are more likely to re-

turn sooner if you stay calm, and your expression of frustration, though understandable, may increase the likelihood of his taking his anger out on the infant.

What can you do? Verbally recognize that Jonathan must feel frightened and upset about the change in the family. With a warm hug, tell him reassuringly that he is loved and valued. In addition, you could ask, "Are you surprised that you're going in your pants again? What do you make of it?" You may be astonished by his answer.

2. *Let your preschooler act out the role reversal.* Our kids managed to dramatize their feelings about their jealousies and their roles unconsciously and without our assistance. Your child may or may not allow herself the full range of her experience and emotions. Here's how you can help her.

If Marta comes to you whining that she can't tie her shoes anymore, you may want to encourage her to explore her wish to return to babyhood. You can say, "I see that you're wanting to feel like a baby again, when I did everything for you. I can understand that since Ali is getting so much attention lately. Now, let's pretend. If you could be a baby again, what would you really like to do?"

Again you might be surprised at your daughter's response:

- She may have a wish to be held and cuddled frequently.
- She may want you to sing to her when you tuck her in at night, the way you do with her sister.
- She may want you to throw her up in the air to make her giggle, the way you do with her sister.
- She may ask for a bottle of milk to suck on.
- She may want to try out new sleeping arrangements in the crib.

If your child's requests can be accommodated easily, there is no harm in doing so, provided that they are not hurtful to herself or others. In fact, fulfilling her requests may ease a portion of the pain that she is feeling and can eliminate the sense of taboo that surrounds her regression. Indeed, when you allow your preschooler to act out her fantasy, it loses its powerful hold on her. She may soon tire of the confinement of the crib or the necessity to carry the bottle around and go on with her more grown-up life.

If you deny your preschooler the opportunity to act out her safe fantasy, the innocent acts that she may wish to engage in can take on a magical power in her mind—if only she could have a bottle again then everything would be all right. She may take out her frustration and her anger on the baby.

If the fantasy involves hurting the baby, that wish, of course, cannot be granted. However, you child can release the anger that lies behind the destructive wish in many different ways. If Mary says, "I wish Scott was never born," you could respond, "I can see that you're angry about having a new brother." Then you can encourage her to

- take it out on a baby doll—let her playact her feelings toward you and her sibling.
- hit a punching bag—this is great for releasing pent-up anger. "You can hit the bag but not your brother."
- draw a picture of what she would like to do to the baby.
- act out her feelings with puppets. (We used a "Cookie Monster" puppet but called him "the Attention Monster." Cherie was able, in that way, to act out her insatiable hunger for mother's attention.)
- play with clay. She can squish and twist the clay. The activity releases anger while it lets her express how she fantasizes treating her new rival.
- pound a mound of pillows with a tennis racket. This make a wonderful loud noise and helps to vent anger.
- wring a towel, which is a great tension reliever.

After the anger has found some safe expression, your child will be more open to accepting, for the while, her sibling.

3. *What if your preschooler asks to nurse at the breast?* If this is not repugnant to you, you may allow him to do so as well. Chances are he'll find the bitterness of mother's milk less appetizing than he fantasized and certainly less delicious than what he has become accustomed to drinking. If he is startled and confused by the bitter taste coupled with baby's obvious pleasure at nursing, you can remind him that since baby has tasted nothing else in her short lifetime, this tastes good to her. As a result, he may appreciate how far he has come.

If breast feeding is repugnant to you, you might say, "I don't feel OK about your nursing on my breast. Would you like a bottle of formula while I hold you close to me?" The next time you can offer to hold him close, without the bottle. In either case, it's important to discuss how he has grown and changed.

All of these suggestions help you to nip discipline problems in the bud by defusing them before they become explosive. But what if your kids are already fighting? How do you get them to stop so that everyone feels like a winner?

THE PRIZEFIGHTERS

Has the following scenario ever happened in your home?

Cherie and Aimee share a room. Cherie is six and Aimee is three. Cherie has set up an elaborate doll village complete with school, store, house, and park, using her imagination and all the toys she can find. However, she has ignored, for the moment, the stuffed-animal collection in the corner by her bed.

Aimee wanders in and wants to be part of the fun. This is natural. The game is awfully tempting. Cherie won't hear of it, however. She is awfully rejecting of her sister, as usual. She says, "These are my dolls. Go away. Go do something else."

Hard pressed, Aimee looks around the room. She spies the abandoned stuffed animals. Although they seem less exciting than her sister's game, she resigns herself to her fate. She plops down in the middle of the toys and begins to construct a rudimentary imaginary village of her own.

Cherie can't tolerate this. She jumps up and runs over to where her sister is playing. "No fair!" she yells. "You're copying my idea. You're just a copycat. Give me my Snoopy. Those are my animals! You have no right to play with them." With that, she tries to grab the toy out of Aimee's hands while she scoops as many of the other stuffed animals as she can muster with her free arm.

As you would expect, Aimee doesn't take this well. She yells back, "I can play if I want to. No. Mine. I want it. Mommy. Mommeeeee." The girls struggle over possession of the animals.

Cherie, being stronger, wins the tug-of-war. As Susan responds to the cries and runs into their room, she witnesses Cherie hitting her younger sister over the head with the stuffed Snoopy. Both of them are crying. Mother feels like a miserable failure.

What would you do if you were in Susan's position? No, this is not a quiz. Just a reenactment of every parent's frustration. How do you resolve it? That's what the rest of this chapter is all about.

HELPING YOUR CHILDREN SETTLE THEIR OWN ARGUMENTS

While sibling rivalry and arguments among children can't be avoided, there are ways to lessen their pain, intensity, and frequency. Try to help your kids work our their own resolutions without resorting to physical or emotional violence. When they find their own way, they are more apt to stick to the solution that they've come up with. They feel less resentment about the consequence because they have chosen it themselves.

How can you help your kids work out their own problems? Here are some suggestions that can help:

1. *Decide if you should intervene.* When are your kids playing, and when are they fighting? It's difficult to give an unequivocal answer here because sometimes it's hard to tell. A tickle fight, for example, can degenerate into meanness and tears if allowed to go on for too long. It's a fine line of demarcation, but you'll know instinctively when your kids have gone beyond the limit. The tone of voice changes. The laughter suddenly sounds hysterical. The tension builds. Some parents can take more dissension than others. Trust your own instincts.

In the case of Aimee, Cherie, and the stuffed animals, Susan heard the raised voices but assumed that the girls were just arguing it out. She was right, at first. And it's OK to allow your kids to do that, as long as they're not abusing each other verbally or physically. Fighting it out, on the other hand, is not acceptable. That's when you'll need to step in.

What would you do in this situation? The girls are lying on opposite ends of the couch. They start playing footsie with each other. That is, each one with legs outstretched is pressing against the feet of the other. It's a fun game. But then one foot slips and lands on the crotch of the other girl. Ouch! That deserves retaliation. A kick to the neck is delivered. Then another to the thigh. All-out combat ensues. In the meantime, Susan is in the kitchen, trying to tutor a doctoral student in French grammar. She hears the giggling stop, and the voices turn tense. The game has escalated past the point of play. Would you intervene?

Bear in mind when you're deciding whether or not to step in that it's important for your kids to attempt to work out their own problems as much as they can. If you intervene all the time, they will never learn how to settle disputes themselves or even that they are capable of settling fights without you. Be judicious with your intervention, but don't hesitate if your gut response is "That doesn't sound like playing to me."

2. *If they are endangering each other, call a halt to the hostility.* Your first priority is to stop your kids from hurting each other.

- Don't rush in and ask, "Who started it?"
- Don't take sides.
- Don't undermine yourself with weak statements like "You kids need to stop now, OK?" You're not asking their permission.
- Don't tell them that your expect your children not to fight and that they're bad for carrying on.
- Just yell, "Stop!" as loud as you can.

Once Susan assessed the stuffed-animal situation after rushing into Cherie and Aimee's room, she simply yelled, "Stop! I'm not going to let you hurt each other!" That got the girls' attention and caused them to drop their weapons for the moment. If you must, physically pull the combatants apart.

3. *Use a time-out.* After you have disengaged the warring factions, separate them by putting them in different rooms. Since our daughters shared their room, Susan evicted both of them from the emotionally charged space. Neither of them got the time-out in the bedroom where they could continue to play. Cherie took her time-out in the kitchen, while Aimee stayed in the living room. Susan asked both girls to think about what happened so they could talk about it later.

4. *Help your child take responsibility for his or her actions.* This can be tough. Kids are most likely to say, "She started it," or "It's her fault." Avoid taking sides. When someone is provoked, there is often a provocateur. Usually, both kids contribute to the problem in some unconscious way.

Begin by getting each child's version of the incident privately. Simply ask, "What happened?" In our case, Cherie said, "I was playing with my toys, and Aimee came in and started to bother me. Mommy, I told her to go away, but she wouldn't. She started playing with my animals. You know how I arranged them just the way I like them. She had no right to touch my animals. She started it. Tell her to leave my stuff alone."

Susan mirrored Cherie's feelings. "Cherie," she said, "I understand why you were angry. It's hard when Aimee uses your things without your permission. But what was your part in all of this? Why have I given you a time-out?"

"I don't know. Because we were fighting, I guess."

"That's right. It's OK to be angry about your sister touching your special things, but it's not OK to hurt her. I won't let you do that. Use your words. Come to me, if you have to, but no hitting."

The same scene repeated itself with Aimee. "She hit me. She called me a copycat. I'm not a copycat. I was playing my own game. She always gets to play with everything, and I never do. She never lets me play with her. Why can't I play with her animals?"

Now Susan mirrored to her younger daughter. "I know it's hard when your sister won't let you play with her. You feel left out. But why do you think I gave you a time-out?"

"Because I took her toys?"

"That's right. It's not OK to take someone else's things without their giving you permission—even if they're not playing with them. You wouldn't like it if she took your Teddy without asking, would you?"

Aimee could see her mother's point.

Then Mother said. "Let's see if we can't find a way to work this out." She called both girls back into their room.

5. *Encourage the children to create their own solution.* In their book *Siblings Without Rivalry*, authors Adele Faber and Elaine

Mazlish suggest a wonderful way to help your children come to some consensus. Parents, they said, should, "express faith in their [children's] ability to work out a mutually agreeable solution. [Then] leave the room."

How did that work in our family? Susan talked to both girls at once. "Aimee and Cherie, this is a difficult problem. But I know that you two can find a way to work this out between you. I'm going to leave so you can figure it out for yourselves."

The girls are called upon to tap into their nobler selves. How do they manage? They do just fine.

"Can I play with your stuffed animals?" Aimee ventured.

"Well, you know I don't like you to," her sister replied.

"I'll let you use my castle for your game if you let me play with them."

"Well, OK, but only if you promise to put them back exactly the way you found them."

"OK. I promise."

Before long, there is a trail of stuffed animals leading to the doll village. Both girls have managed to find a way to play with each other.

A CASE IN POINT

These same girls, as teenagers, were able to apply the principles we've just discussed to their own lives without our intervention.

After many months of their intrusion into our phone lines, we decided it was time for them to have their own line. After the rejoicing died down (on both sides), the girls came up against a potential area of great conflict. What if both of them wanted to use the phone at the same time?

We told them that since it was their phone, we were not going to interfere. We trusted them to come up with a solution that they could both live with. And they did. If one sister was on the phone and the other needed to use it, the first sister had to relinquish the line within fifteen minutes. With the addition of the call-waiting option, incoming calls were also part of the agreement. If the incoming call was for the other sister, it was treated as a call she needed to make. The fifteen-minute rule still applied.

This system has worked reasonably well, although there were some breakdowns around the time of Cherie's senior prom, when she just had to work out the details, and at the time of final exams, when Aimee held marathon study sessions on the phone. By working the rules out themselves in advance, the girls couldn't come back to us to complain if they suddenly perceived the system as being unfair. If they wanted to make changes, it was up to them.

Our daughters came up with this solution themselves after many years of conflict resolution. It made us feel proud of their ability to be flexible and to reach a consensus. But we also recognized that their increasingly friendly relationship was a product of working on sibling-rivalry issues over the years. In order to weaken the potential for conflict, it's important to understand why your kids fight and how you can use their emotional pain to help them grow in satisfying ways.

■ ■ ■

Feeling Good About Discipline
GUIDE TO CURBING SIBLING ARGUMENTS

1. Become aware of your own experiences with your parents and siblings because your history can influence
   - how much and in what way you empathize with your children;
   - the methods and approach you use for discipline.
2. Siblings fight because of jealousy.
3. Use fantasy play to help your children to act out regression:
   - Regression is a sign that your child needs your help in dealing with an important issue.
     - Don't criticize your preschooler for regression.
     - Let your preschooler act out the role reversal.
4. If your preschooler's angry at a sibling, guide him toward releasing his anger in a safe, creative way.
5. Help your children to settle their own arguments:
   - Decide if you should intervene by using the "That doesn't sound like play to me," yardstick.
   - Call an immediate halt to hostility.
   - Use a time-out.
   - Help your children to take responsibility for their actions.
   - Encourage your children to create their own solutions.

CHAPTER THIRTEEN

Sometimes It's Better for Him to Cry Than for You to Cry

RECENTLY A MOTHER in Colorado wrote a letter to "Dear Abby" that echoes what we believe about disciplining preschoolers. "I am deeply disturbed by something I see every day on the streets and roads," she began.

"Last week I was driving behind a couple in a sports vehicle. A boy, who could not have been more than three years old, was with them, standing in the back seat with his head halfway out the window.

"I am a mother and know what it's like to have your child cry and tell you that you're mean because you want the child strapped in a car seat. But believe me, I would much rather hear my child cry and be upset for a few minutes than to lie awake at night asking God to forgive me for causing his death by giving in because he didn't want to be strapped in. . . .

"I would like to tell every parent in the world to tell the child who is resisting being buckled in. 'No, you cannot ride without being buckled in. I love you too much to endanger you.'"

This closely approximates an incident in Susan's life when she was only five years old.

Susan was a rambunctious, energetic child. One day, she stood waiting on the corner for her mother to pick her up from kindergarten. She knew very well not to cross the street. On this day, however, she couldn't contain herself. As soon as she saw her mom coming up the hill, she took off to greet her. She ran across the street all by herself without looking both ways as she had been taught. Several cars screeched to a halt in order not to hit her.

When Susan got to her destination, she had a surprise in store. Rather than the hug and kiss she expected, her mom grabbed her by one arm and gave her a sound spanking right there on the street corner in front of her friends. Much wailing and crying ensued, mostly out of embarrassment.

After they got home, and both had a chance to calm down a bit, Susan and her mother talked about what had happened.

"Susie, you know that what you did was wrong."

"Yes, I shouldn't have run across without looking," she admitted.

"You also should have waited for me to hold your hand while you crossed," her mother added.

"But why did you spank me like that?"

"I wanted to teach you a lesson," her mother replied. "When I saw those cars coming at you, I was sure you were going to get hit. Imagine how I felt. And imagine how you would have felt if the cars couldn't stop. It would have hurt you a lot more than my spanking. I'm going to tell you something my mother used to say to me when I was a child and did something dangerous. In a case like this, *it's better for you to cry than for me to cry.*"

Susan thought about what her mother had said. Although she didn't like the idea, she could see that her mother had a point. After all, what would make her mother cry? Her injury or death. Even though she didn't fully understand those concepts, the ideas were pretty scary possibilities. The lesson stayed with her for a lifetime. She was also much more careful about crossing the street.

We incorporated *it's better for him to cry than for you to cry* into our disciplinary style when we became parents. It seemed reasonable to us, since some decisions our kids made were inappropriate and downright dangerous.

Once Cherie was about to investigate the interior of a wall socket with a bobby pin. That was in the days before professional babyproofing came into vogue. Today industry has recognized the rightness of our anxiety with the invention of those handy little socket covers. We had no such aid twenty-five years ago. A sharp slap on the hand coupled with a loud "No! Hot!" got the idea across quickly. Cherie didn't like it. Too bad. The alternative was much worse.

Sometimes an emergency will warrant your inflicting a slap on the hand as we have occasionally felt it necessary to do. There may be no time to discuss the pros and cons of a particular action. Your child needs to get the message immediately, for the sake of his own safety.

At other times, however, your preschooler will cry out of anger and frustration because he did not get his way even when no physical punishment has been administered. You're not going to argue with Andrew about why he should stay out of the household cleaners under the sink, which he managed—despite all of your precautions—to find access to. You want him away from there now, and you want him never to touch the poisons again. Period. Whether he likes your ruling or not should not deter your resolve. There's no harm in letting him cry about it. Better him than you.

Kids play with matches, try to go swimming in the backyard pool by themselves, chase their errant balls into traffic, and climb to dizzying heights on kitchen counters to search for goodies in the cupboards. You name it, and your curious, energetic preschooler will try it. After all, he's only doing his job—he's out to learn about the world and how it works.

But that means that you have to do your job, too. Protect him so that he'll live to see adulthood. Be firm when he gets into danger. And don't let his tears manipulate you into acquiescing to his wishes. You may hurt him more by giving in.

Even when there is no imminent danger but only the possibility of harm, you have a right to make your limits very clear, regardless of your preschooler's feelings about it. For example, your children are playing in the backseat of the car as you take them to the daycare center. They get into a tickle fight. But you can see that the older one is getting the upper hand. It doesn't sound like fun anymore; it sounds like harassment. You feel that you must keep turning around to referee while you're driving. You give one warning: "If you guys don't settle down, I'm going to pull over and move Josh to the front seat."

"But I don't want to move," he whines. "We're having fun."

"It's hard for me to concentrate on driving when you are carrying on in the back. I need it relatively calm. I know that you don't want to move, but I'm afraid we'll have an accident if this keeps up. Kevin is in his car seat, and it's harder for me to move him. So just cool it."

If the kids continue their disruptive game, make good on your promise, despite pleas to the contrary. It's better for them to cry about not getting their way than for you to cry after the aftermath of a car accident.

WHAT ABOUT HITTING?

Let's be realistic. Almost every parent that Mitch has worked with has spanked, shaken, or slapped their child at one point or another. The parents usually feel very guilty about it later. And yet, in truth, in some of those situations, they saw no other alternative. Are these parents bad or abusive?

The answer isn't clear. Do we advocate hitting? Absolutely not. However, occasionally, in a real or imagined desperate situation, a slap on the hand may be appropriate as a way to convey extreme danger quickly. This slap is not a solution. It's a way to get your preschooler's full attention. Once the crisis is over, it provides you with the opportunity to discuss with your child what happened, so that it won't happen again. During your discussion, you can incorporate a consequence for such a future dangerous misbehavior.

Spanking, as Susan remembered, is humiliating. Of course, if you can use consequences instead, you'll all be better off.

Let us be perfectly clear, however. A slap on the hand as an immediate attention grabber in a moment of grave danger is different from regular and frequent use of spanking, hitting, or beating. Hitting with objects that can inflict physical harm, such as belts, sticks, or shoes, is clearly abusive. This practice is unacceptable and is subject to investigation by child-protective services and the police.

We are talking about very specific situations where there is a clear and present danger. Children learn about the concept of hot immediately after they touch a flame. We don't want them to learn about cars and streets in the same way!

Hitting children as a punishment is unacceptable and emotionally damaging. When children are out of control, some parents believe that they can gain the upper hand by hitting them. These parents respond out of their own feelings of frustration. Hitting seems to work initially, since it gets the child to stop for the moment. But parents have to inflict more and more punishment over time in order for this kind of disciplining to seem effective. That's not a desired goal. And it's not effective. For one thing, it tells the child that violence is a way of resolving problems. This increases his own violent behavior. Language skills, internal controls, and conscience get lost in the shuffle.

Besides, such escalating spanking could work its way into child abuse. Indeed, the whole system breaks down at adolescence when parents feel that their children are too old or too big to hit. At this point, parents often relinquish their discipline responsibilities to school authorities or to the police.

It's better for him to cry than for you to cry is not a carte blanche for us to hit our children every time we feel upset or uncomfortable. Hitting is not "a convenience" for us to use to relieve our own frustrations. The important point is that there are other effective ways to set limits and change behavior.

WHEN YOU MAKE A MISTAKE

Sometimes we spank our kids out of our own fears. We have all heard the horror stories of preschoolers choking on toys, being electrocuted, drowning in swimming pools and even bath tubs, or getting hit by cars. Our overcompensation is automatic and human.

Or we may simply overreact to a benign situation. Some parents scream if their preschooler spills his milk, plays with his shoelaces, or mucks around with the dirt in a flowerpot. This overreaction is not the end of the world. There is no perfect parenting, nor are there perfect parents. Everyone makes mistakes, including, as you have seen, "the experts." In fact, throughout this book we have shared our own foibles with you as a way of reassuring you that even though mistakes will happen, you can still be effective parents. Indeed, your children will use your errors as a way to separate from you and create their own lives as they grow into adulthood. It's part of their evolutionary development.

And if on further reflection, you feel that you have gone too far, don't be afraid to admit your mistake to your child. A simple "I'm sorry. I was scared. I didn't mean to hurt you," or "I'm sorry. I'm nervous today. I didn't mean to yell at you," coupled with a warm hug and expressions of your love, will go a long way in easing his pain and letting him know that you can make mistakes and amends, too.

THE VALUE OF YOUR CHILD'S TEARS

Rarely are problems life threatening, as were Susan's running across the street and Cherie's exploration of the electrical socket. But even less dangerous painful experiences teach your children valuable life lessons.

Mitch learned his the hard way, too. When he was four years old, he offered to carry a neighbor's watermelon up the stairs to her apartment. He liked Mrs. Block, and he loved her cocker spaniel puppy, Spanky. He often played with Mrs. Block's daughter, who suffered from cerebral palsy. He thought that since he was such a "big boy," he could help the family easily with his act of largess. He bragged about his strength and prowess. "I'm just like the Lone Ranger," he said boastfully.

Mitch's mother warned him not to take on something that he couldn't handle: "You won't be helping Mrs. Block if you drop the watermelon. It's very heavy. And if you can't manage it, and it falls and breaks, you'll have to pay for it."

"No, no," Mitch insisted excitedly. "I can do it. I can do it."

Pretending he was his famous hero, Mitch strained to pick up the heavy melon. He steadied it on his shoulder and felt triumphant. "You see," he called. "I did it."

He was right. He could hold it. But he sure couldn't walk with it. He took several steps toward Mrs. Block's apartment and lost his balance. That was fatal. As he felt the melon slipping out of his grasp, he burst into tears. His inflated hopes were as broken as the remnants of smashed fruit lying at his feet.

Children face disappointments all the time. Tears, pain, and consequences are all a part of growing up. Tears are one way your child comes to terms with the world. They inform him that

- the world can be dangerous.
- things happen beyond our control.

- we are not all-powerful, as we would like to believe.
- life is sometimes very difficult.
- we can't always have our way.

These valuable albeit painful lessons teach your children how to function in the real world. They help them to understand the risks, frailty, and limitedness that we all must live with.

This is not to say that we should rub our kids' noses in their disappointments as if they were erring puppies. We can be understanding of our children's pain while not relenting in what we believe is in their best interest. Use mirroring expressions such as

- "I know you want to go swimming, but I'm not going to let you go into the pool when you have an ear infection."
- "I know you want to stay up late, but tomorrow you have to get up early for nursery school. If you don't get enough sleep, you may get sick again."
- "I know you're hungry now, but I'm not going to let you eat candy so close to lunchtime. Have a carrot or an apple."
- "I realize that sometimes it's hard for you to share your new toys with your friends, but why don't you see if you can find a way to work this out between you?"

These expressions lend support and validation to your child's feelings without giving in to inappropriate behavior. Your child's response of crying or pain at being denied his wishes is a normal part of life. You certainly don't get everything that you want. Why raise him with the false expectation that he can? He's bound to feel resentment and frustration when he discovers that the rest of the world does not respond to his demands the way that you do.

■ ■ ■

Feeling Good About Discipline
WHEN IS IT BETTER FOR HIM TO CRY
THAN FOR YOU TO CRY?

1. Sometimes a slap on the hand is warranted, especially when your child is in extreme danger.
2. Use the occasion to discuss with your child the danger of the situation and an appropriate consequence for such a future activity.
3. Your preschooler may cry when you frustrate his desires. Stick to your guns, especially if you perceive that he has made a dangerous or inappropriate decision.
4. Regular hitting, spanking, or beating
   ■ is physically harmful and dangerous in itself.
   ■ is ineffectual in the long run.
   ■ teaches your child that violence is an acceptable way to settle problems.
   ■ can work its way into child abuse since it must escalate.
5. Apologize if you have overreacted or made a mistake. Work at changing your approach.
6. Reasonable frustration, tears, and consequence (we're not talking about deprivation or child abuse here) can help to prepare your preschooler for a complex world.
7. Use mirroring to help assuage frustration.

CHAPTER FOURTEEN

Disciplining Your Preschooler in a Two-Career Family

As THE PARENTS of a preschooler in this day and age, chances are you are both part of the work force, and that can present certain dilemmas in dealing with your youngster that your own parents may not have had to face. For example, you may feel the pressure of time—you never have enough of it to do everything you must and still have fun with your kids. As a result, you may have difficulty saying no to your preschooler's demands because you feel guilty or don't want to alienate her. (See Chapter 1 on why kids want and need discipline.)

We recently saw this dynamic in action while we were at a local mall, window shopping as we waited for the movie theater to empty for the 10:00 P.M. show. It was a Sunday evening, and all the stores were closed and locked. As we strolled around, we came across a young family: mother, father, and four-year-old daughter. The preschooler had stopped in front of a store selling Disney memorabilia, and she was not budging.

"I wanna go in," she cried, rattling the door.

"But, Chelsea," her dad replied in as calm a tone as he could muster, "Mickey and Minnie, and Snow White, and Cinderella, and Pocahantas, and Hercules are all asleep. It's dark inside. We'll come back next week when the store is open."

Chelsea, however was not to be consoled, especially since "next week" didn't mean much to her. "I wanna go in. I wanna go in," she wailed, her demands becoming increasingly shrill.

We could see that this youngster's parents were discomfited by the racket but were hard pressed to know what to do about it. They glanced at each other and seemed to alternate between trying to ignore their daughter's outbursts (and resume their now disrupted good time) and pulling her away from her post (which would have probably provoked a full-blown tantrum).

We continued on. Although we didn't witness how this family solved its problem, it occurred to us that some deeper issues might have been at work here. We wondered, for instance, what pressures these parents must have felt to find themselves taking a leisurely walk with such a young child at 9:45 in the evening in the first place. A darkened, semi-deserted mall seemed an inappropriate venue for a four-year-old late on a Sunday evening. We imagined that they were torn between whether it was better to spend "quality time" together or have their daughter in bed.

Moreover, because of this conflict, it seemed to us that these parents were struggling to get straightforward limits: "The store is closed. We can't go in right now," or "Let's go home. It's time for you to go to sleep, too." They treated their daughter as if they were handling eggshells, and the tension in their voices was almost palpable.

Unfortunately, sometimes working parents' understandable desire to be with their children and their guilt over not doing so interferes with their ability to fulfill their youngster's needs for structure and routine. This conflict between quality time and setting limits often leads to indulgences that parents recognize as wrong. They feel guilty for letting their kids stay up too late, snack on junk food and soda, or watch too much television. Nevertheless, they may give in to their youngsters' every demand to compensate for their absence.

So what could Chelsea's parents have done in the mall? The simplest approach would probably have been to say, "Chelsea, the store is closed. It's not OK for you to stand there shaking the door and yelling. If you don't come here and hold my hand we'll have to go right home. You have a choice: more walking or home. Which will it be?"

Of course, depending on Chelsea's decision, these parents would continue on their stroll or head straight for the parking lot, screaming child in tow. Although consistent follow-through might have created some discomfort for them all, it would have taught Chelsea that her parents care enough about her to create safe boundaries and limits for her behavior, whether or not they feel guilty about being gone so much.

DIVIDING THE CHORES

The two-career families that Mitch counsels clearly recognize that setting limits is the solution to their problems with their preschoolers. But before dealing with the issue of limits, Mitch has found that two-career couples may need to work out an equitable division of labor when it comes to child-rearing.

Research has shown that spouses often have expectations of equality as they await the arrival of their first child. But once the infant is born, men and women fall back into timeworn patterns of behavior; on the whole mothers occupy themselves with their children's bodily needs (meals, baths, pediatrician visits) while fathers play and enjoy unstructured activities like rough-housing and tossing a ball around.

Unfortunately, despite everyone's best intentions, mothers still do more of the parenting than fathers, and they may feel overwhelmed by the dual burden of work and home. They may need to build into their daily routine some equitable "off time" so that they don't take out their frustrations on their children by overindulging them.

We have found that the easiest way to create a more equitable division of labor is to list, prioritize, and schedule parenting tasks appropriate for sharing, such as bathing the kids, reading them storybooks, dropping them off at preschool, or preparing them for bedtime. You can each choose favorite activities while you divide the less enjoyable tasks fairly between you. You may even want to set up a weekly calendar of involvements, charting your parenting activities for the sake of clarity until they become routine. Be flexible and plan for trade-offs and further negotiation as the situation warrants. Your plan may change as your family needs evolve.

Your chart will create a sense of orderliness in your household. And, whether or not you are full-time attorneys or full-time stay-at-home parents, your children will feel most safe when you create a structured environment. Finally, adhering to the principles of disciplining with love that we have advocated throughout this book reinforces that feeling of safety.

RITUALS ARE ESSENTIAL

Young children need consistent patterns and structured rituals (in the morning, at mealtime, story time, and bedtime, for instance) that they can depend on to help them feel safe.

It's important not to disrupt your preschooler's rituals to compensate for your own feelings of missing your kids.

Conflicting needs and the disruption of rituals cropped up in a two-career family Mitch was seeing in his practice. Before Russ and Sharon had had kids, they had enjoyed a certain measure of unstructured adult playtime after work. They took walks together in the early evening. On nights when Russ went to play basketball with his pals, Sharon hit the gym and worked out on the stationary bike and the weight machines. Somehow this couple had nurtured the expectation that they would continue their routine after their son was born. But, as we all know by now, children have a way of disrupting their parents' best-laid plans.

Once Timmy arrived, it was nearly impossible for Russ and Sharon to play as they had become used to doing. When Timmy reached the age of three, his mom and dad felt it feasible to return to their old pursuits, at least on a limited basis. However, for either parent to get out of the house for some unstructured leisure activity meant that the other one had sole duty at home—a babysitter was rarely available midweek or, for that matter, affordable.

This worked for a while, but after several weeks Russ and Sharon each began to feel resentful of being the single-duty parent during his or her evenings "on." Moreover, they received a disturbing report from Timmy's preschool teacher.

"He seems so tired all the time," the teacher said when Russ came to pick up his son one day. "Yesterday, he fell asleep right in the middle of story time. Usually he just loves those stories. And when he's so cranky, he has a hard time getting along with the other kids. Today he tried to bite Marcie. I was wondering, has there been a change of routine in the family?"

Sharon and Russ had to reevaluate. Out of their need to take care of themselves, they had stretched Timmy's bedtime beyond what was comfortable or salutary for him. For example, when Sharon returned from the gym, she felt re-vitalized and ready to play with her son. She had been ask-ing her husband to keep Timmy up because otherwise she would have had no time with him at all. Although Timmy would usually be winding down at the moment, the appear-ance of his energized mother stimulated him to play more. Because Russ also expected his son to stay up on nights he was out playing ball, Timmy's bedtime was delayed and un-predictable.

Sharon and Russ loved their son and wanted to be able to give him quality time. Nevertheless, they had forgotten that young children need structure, rituals, and consistency in or-der to feel safe. Mitch reminded them of the importance of observing their youngster's bedtime rituals, no matter what their own needs were. Russ and Sharon were adults and could adjust. Timmy, on the other hand, was still a child, and he was losing out. At the very least, he needed to be put to bed on time with his usual bedtime story and hug.

OFFSETTING THE INFLUENCE OF YOUR WORK ENVIRONMENT

Of course, work has an impact on you too. Some parents come home from their labors so exhausted that they feel they haven't the energy to set limits with their kids. They know they should be more consistent, but they give in to their youngsters' demands. Like a punch-drunk boxer at the end of a fight, they would do anything to avoid more tension.

Other parents become used to the highly structured en-vironment at work in which roles are defined and relation-ships, for the most part, are hierarchical. Tasks have a be-ginning, middle, and end, and time is planned and organized. It may be difficult for these parents to shift gears into an en-vironment that's unstructured and free-floating. They may expect their youngsters to respond to them as they would their employees or subordinates. If parents do bark out orders, they may feel guilty later and compensate by being overly indulgent.

On the other hand, walking into a household right after work can tax even the calmest soul. Children are usually cranky and needy during the late afternoon. They miss their parents and demand attention. For the parents, though, there's mail to open, dinner to prepare, and the day's happenings to catch up on.

If you feel that your work is impacting your ability to parent, a family meeting (see Chapter 4) may be useful in prioritizing your activities. You may also find it helpful to give yourself a time-out when you get home. We've adapted the following suggestions from our book *Finding Time for Fathering* to help ease the transition from work to home. These are applicable to both fathers and mothers:

1. *If at all possible, take a few minutes to yourself before interacting with your family.* In our household, Susan came home from work long before Mitch did. She had a few hours alone with Cherie and Aimee before he arrived. So we resolved that Mitch not be disturbed for twenty minutes after he walked in the door. He greeted everyone and then went into our bedroom for a nap. Once rested, he put in some time with our kids and gave Susan a twenty minute break.

Other families in Mitch's practice have devised different strategies. One mom parked down the block and played a relaxation tape in her car before braving the home front. One father simply sat in his car outside his daughter's preschool for ten minutes, collecting his thoughts before picking her up. You can also use meditations, relaxation tapes, and classical music to help create a break between work and home.

2. *Play with your children for five minutes and then take a nap.* If your kids are not old enough to tolerate the frustration

of your absence right away, play with them for a short time as soon as you walk in the door. Then, promise more play-time later when you're feeling better (after your nap). Take turns doing this with your spouse if you both arrive home simultaneously.

3. *Use music or a story tape as a timing device.* A preschooler may not be able to comprehend how long fifteen minutes is. But you can set up a tape recorder with favorite songs or stories and say, "When this tape is over, I'll come out and play with you." This helps your child gauge and adjust to the separation. A timer may work too, but it's less fun. While your youngster is listening, you can grab a catnap or talk with your spouse.

4. *Take a few minutes with your spouse just to ventilate.* While your youngster is listening to the tape, set up a time for mutual whining with your spouse. Assign yourself five minutes each to complain about your day. Neither of you has to feel obligated to do anything about the other's stress. You're just trading war stories. Then you can settle into the evening activities with your youngsters more peacefully.

DEALING WITH YOUR PRESCHOOLER IF YOU WORK AT HOME

More and more parents work at home and keep in touch with their office or clients through a fax machine and computer modem. You may find yourself spending long hours working at home as an independent real estate broker, attorney, handyman, publicist, freelance writer, professor, student, or artist. One of the advantages of working at home is the freedom to regulate your own schedule. One of the disadvantages is that you're always at work *and* you're always at home. The demarcation between family time and business is not so clearly drawn.

Even though your youngest is around, you may need privacy to accomplish your work or, for safety reasons (and your sanity), you may need him to stay away from your computer or other work-related tools or papers. You may find it painful to be so close to your child yet so unavailable. If your preschooler demands attention, you can try to build him into your work activities as your explain what your work entails.

First, it's best to set up ground rules, including designated workspace areas that are either child-friendly or off-limits. You can explain to your child that he's free to visit when your door is open, but once you've closed it, he can't interrupt. Be sure to set up consequences and to follow through consistently. If you're continually disturbed by family squabbles, however, the garage may be a more distant and suitable workplace.

Also keep in mind that you're actually on three-quarters time. Distractions and intrusions are bound to occur so it's best to expect them and even plan for them. But let's face it, even in an office you're often interrupted by related but tangential phone calls and coworkers' concerns. Some home-offce parents use interactions with their kids as planned breaks from more cerebral activities. You can make a 4:00 P.M. date with your son for fifteen minutes of finger painting or with your daughter for fifteen minutes at her tea party. They'll be delighted and you'll feel refreshed. Make a ritual of your time together.

It's also possible to allow your preschooler to share your workspace for limited periods of time. Let your child play with his blocks next to your desk, where he'll be able to reassure himself of your presence from time to time. He can paint quietly on the floor for ten minutes or look at picture books.

If your child is interested and able to understand, engage her in a discussion and demonstration of what you're working on. Show her how to send a fax or push the button on the light meter for your camera equipment. Let her sit on your lap in front of the computer and do some "writing." She will find the opportunity to participate in your work stimulating and exciting. But be sure to explain the rules governing the touching of your equipment when you're away.

INCLUDING YOUR KIDS IN YOUR WORK

Rather than indulging your children, it's far better to include them in your work. All in all, getting your preschooler involved in your work will help bring your family closer while assuaging some of your guilt over taking time away from parenting responsibilities. Moreover, it has positive implications in your child's development: the more contact with you, the better her social, emotional, intellectual, and sex-role development.

How do you include your preschooler in a meaningful way? The following suggestions, adapted from *Finding Time for Fathering*, may help you do just that.

Photographs. Take photos of your workplace. (If your job is in a restricted area, photos of the lobby or other public areas will work too.) Have a coworker take a snapshot of you on the job. Take pictures of coworkers and of the cafeteria and the restrooms. (Preschoolers are interested in body functions and where you take care of them!)

When you bring these photos home to your youngster, say, "I just want to show you where I go each day." You child can keep scrapbooks called *Where My Dad Works* or *Where My Mom Works* and, depending on her age, she can add text explaining where you are and what you're doing. Your preschooler will refer to this scrapbook in your absence as a way of connecting to you.

In addition, give your child a picture of you affectionately holding her as a reminder of your love for each other. Your youngster can store this keepsake in her cubby at school or in her room at home and will look at it when she misses you. If you have a video camera, simply turn it on yourself and your work environment.

Bring Your Work Home. Bring home a part of work that your youngster can understand. If you've designed a fabulous new stapler, show her the mock-up or the blueprints; if you're a physician, let her listen to your heart, then her heart with a stethoscope; if you're engaged in manufacture, bring home a finished product to show.

Found Objects. Sometimes your work is relatively intangible—your preschooler may have difficulty relating to a life insurance policy—but you can still help her connect to you at work using found objects.

If you work in an office, you can recycle the ends torn from tractor-feed computer paper. These are great for art projects or for stuffing dolls' beds. Empty cartons that had stored reams of copier paper can be put to a hundred uses such as the construction of toy cars, make-believe kitchens, and pretend supermarket shelves. When your preschooler plays with these cast-offs, she will associate them—the smell of the paper, the feel of the cardboard—with you and your work.

An Adventure Excursion to Your Workplace. A trip to your workplace is important because it helps your children visualize and understand how your world is organized. Think about the fun parts of your work from your children's point of view. If you're a lawyer or are engaged in a similar office-centered business, let your kids sit behind your desk and twirl in your swivel chair. They can have great fun with your dictaphone, speeding up or slowing down their recorded voices. They may enjoy watching how the photocopiers or fax machines work. Adding machines that spew forth rolls of tape are also big winners with kids.

If you work in a large factory, you may wish to take your children to one facet of the operation, since the whole plant could be overwhelming or dangerous to a young child.

The following are general suggestions that will make your youngster's visit more successful:

1. *Prepare for the visit.* Before you bring your child into your workplace, check company policy about children visitors. Do they need hardhats or badges? Can they visit after hours or during lunch? If visits are prohibited, difficult, or too dangerous, take a Sunday drive simply to show your youngster where you go every day when you leave for work.

2. *Be available during the visit.* Concrete markers make the work world real for children. Show your child around. Make sure to point out where you park your car, go to the bathroom, hang your clothes, eat, punch in, store your tools, work. Introduce your preschooler to your coworkers. Help her to observe the safety rules. If possible, let her "help out." She can sit at the desk or "try" the cash register. Take photos of the visit showing both of you at work. Depending on your child's age and attention span, try to keep the visit short and sweet, especially the first one. You don't want her to get bored, and you'd like her to be eager to return.

3. *Follow up after the visit.* A question-and-answer recap is an essential part of your excursion. Make sure you ask your youngster what she thinks of your workplace. Ask if *she* has any questions. Have her draw a picture of your workplace and then describe it. If she's too young to write, she can dictate her impressions for you. Discuss photos you might have taken and add these and her drawings to the *Where My Mom Works* scrapbook. In that way, you can amplify the experience so that it lasts many days and weeks.

Disciplining your preschooler can be difficult if you're torn by the many demands of work and family. But with a little planning and forethought and by setting limits and respecting your youngster's rituals, your child will feel safe and will thrive. And that's something you can all feel good about!

206 ■ THORNY PROBLEMS

■ ■ ■

Feeling Good About Discipline
GUIDE TO TWO-CAREER FAMILIES

1. Dual careers may make it hard for you to follow through consistently with limits you've set.
2. Find some ways to divide child care equitably.
   - List and prioritize tasks.
   - Set up a weekly calendar of child-related events.
3. Create rituals around meals and bedtime to help your preschooler feel safe.
4. Take some time for yourself when you first come home.
5. Allow for time with your preschooler if you work at home.
6. If possible, include your children in your work.

Pulling It All Together

When we stick to our disciplining commitment, we are telling our children that we want them to survive and thrive physically and emotionally. Discipline is a kind of caring that helps prepare our children for life. And it is a long-term commitment, not a last-ditch effort to correct a problem that has blown out of all proportion. An integral part of responsible child care, discipline is a way of conveying closeness.

From our experience with children, we have found that when limits are clear and follow-through logical and consistent, our children were less combative. They felt their world was safe and orderly. When a conflict had been resolved to everyone's understanding, if not liking, our daughters were likely to cuddle up to us and give and receive affection. We could all be closer with one another.

Feeling good about discipline implies understanding the underlying need for structure in your children's lives. It also means developing a loving relationship rather than a "perfect" one. Such a human relationship is filled with the complexities of life itself: trials and errors, hopes and fears, failures and successes.

It's perhaps portentous that we competed the discussion and note-taking for the first edition of this book on the way home from driving our oldest daughter to her first semester at the University of California at Santa Cruz. We had reached the pinnacle of parenthood: the moment we had to let go of our child and hope that the lessons we had taught her would serve her well in life. We know that going off to college seems so remote when you're hip deep in potty training and tantrums, but believe us, it does come upon you ever so quickly.

The drive from Los Angeles to Santa Cruz is six hours long. And on the way home we had plenty of time to reflect on the changes that our lives had undergone in the last eighteen years—not to mention the changes that were soon to come with one child out of the house, and the second not far behind.

We also took a moment to ponder the fact that this was the very same road we had traveled that fateful morning thirteen years earlier on our way to Cambria and our adventure with the green peas. Little did we know *then* that our mistakes would be incorporated into a book to help parents deal with their own parenting difficulties. Little did we know that those two curly-haired tots who were giving us so much trouble would grow into two intelligent, responsible, and loving young women (who have come to enjoy being taken out to dinner at the fanciest of restaurants). Look at how far we have come! Isn't life marvelous?

Bibliography

AXLINE, VIRGINIA. *Play Therapy*, Boston: Houghton Mifflin, 1947.

BLOS, PETER. *The Adolescent Passage, Developmental Issues*. New York: International Universities Press, 1979.

BROWN, JOSEPH H. AND CAROLYN S. BROWN. *Systematic Counseling*. Champaign, IL: Research Press Co. 1977.

CANTER, LEE, WITH MARLENE CANTER. *Assertive Discipline*. Los Angeles: Canter and Associates, 1976.

COLM, HANNA. *The Existential Approach to Psychotherapy with Adults and Children*. New York: Grune and Stratton, 1966.

DRIEKURS, RUDOLPH. *Children: The Challenge*. Duell, Sloan, Pearce, 1964.

ERIKSON, ERIK H. *Identity: Youth and Crisis*. New York: W. W. Norton and Company, 1987.

FABER, ADELE, AND ELAINE MAZLISH. *How to Talk So Kids Will Listen & Listen So Kids Will Talk*. New York: Avon Books, 1980.

FABER, ADELE, AND ELAINE MAZLISH. *Siblings Without Rivalry*. New York: Avon Books, 1987.

FLEMING, DON, WITH LINDA BALAHOUTIS. *How to Stop the Battle With Your Child*. West Covina, CA: Don Fleming Seminars Publishing Co., 1982.

GOLANT, MAURICE, C. "Communication Styles That Build." *Fostering the Adolescent: Focus on Relationships and Behavior*. Department of Human Development, Los Angeles: University of California, Los Angeles Extension, 1981.

GOLANT, MITCH, AND SUSAN GOLANT. *Finding Time for Fathering*. New York: Ballantine Books, 1992.

GOLANT, MITCH, AND DONNA CORWIN. *The Challenging Child*. New York: Berkley Books, 1995.

GOLANT, SUSAN K., AND MITCH GOLANT. *Getting Through to Your Kids*. Los Angeles: Lowell House, 1991.

GOLANT, SUSAN K., AND MITCH GOLANT. *Kindergarten: It Isn't What It Used to Be*. Second Edition. Los Angeles: Lowell House, 1997.

GOLEMAN, DANIEL. *Emotional Intelligence*. New York: Bantam Books, 1995.

HOCHSCHILD, ARLIE, WITH ANNE MACHUNG. *The Second Shift: Working Parents and the Revolution at Home*. New York: Viking, 1989.

JONES, RUSSELL A., CLYDE HENDRICK, AND YACOV M. EPSTEIN. *Introduction to Social Psychology*. Sunderland, MA: Sinauer Associates, Inc., 1979.

KUTNER, LAWRENCE. *Parent & Child: Getting Through to Each Other*. New York: William Morrow and Co., 1991.

KOHLBERG, LAWRENCE. "Stage and Sequence: The Cognitive Developmental Approach to Socialization." In *Handbook of Socialization Theory and Research*, edited by D. A. Goslin. Chicago: Rand McNally, 1969.

———. "Moral Stages and Moralization: The Cognitive-Developmental Approach." In *Moral Development and Behavior: Theory, Research and Social Issues,* edited by T. Lickona. New York: Holt, Rinehart and Winston, 1976.

LUDINGTON-HOE, SUSAN, WITH SUSAN K. GOLANT. *How to Have a Smarter Baby*. New York: Bantam Books, 1987.

MACKOFF, BARBARA. *What Mona Lisa Knew: A Woman's Guide to Getting Ahead in Business by Lightening Up*. Los Angeles: Lowell House, 1990.

MAHLER, MARGARET S., F. PINE, AND A. BERGMAN. *The Psychological Birth of the Human Infant*. New York: Basic Books, 1975.

PIAGET, JEAN. *The Moral Development of the Child*. New York: Harcourt, Brace, 1932.

RAPHAEL, BETTE-JEAN. "What's a Nice Couple Like You Doing in a Fight About Discipline?" *Child*. August/September, 1988.

SAMALIN, NANCY, WITH MARTHA MORAGHAN JABLOW. *Loving Your Child is Not Enough: Positive Discipline That Works*. Penguin Books, 1987.

SPOCK, BENJAMIN. *Baby and Child Care*. New York: Pocket Books, 1969.

VAN BUREN, ABIGAIL. "Don't Risk Kids' Lives in Vehicles." *Los Angeles Times*. June 23, 1997.

Index